Sew a Row Quilts

Karin Hellaby

Quilters Haven
Publications

Acknowledgements

This book is dedicated to Mor, my Norwegian mother, who has been and still is such a loving, positive influence in my life.

My three sons are my greatest achievement and it is their needs that focused me to produce this book. My eldest son, Ross, will be starting university in September 2001, followed by Jason and Alexander. I wish to continue to help and support them and hope this book will go some way towards the cost of their higher education.

My thanks to the group of quilters who gathered together on Thursday evenings from mid January 2001 to test the techniques in this book and promised to produce a quilt each by the end of May. Some of them became addicted to the concept and produced two quilts!

I knew 'Sew a Row Quilts' would appeal to new quilters when John Hazon started quilting whilst his wife was out shopping.

John read my instructions and decided to have a go, despite never having sewn before. He had completed several blocks by the time his wife arrived home, but Helen had to explain to him that it would be easier if he used the sewing machine from the right side!

Without the help of Rosemary Muntus, the graphic artist (and sometime quilter!), I would not have achieved the wonderful diagrams I had envisaged but could not draw. Her husband Allan Scott supported us both with his experience in editing.

My two eldest sons are great at educating their Mum in the computer skills needed to bring her into the 21st century – a steep learning curve and often frustrating for all three of us.

I often learn as much from the students I teach as they learn from me. To all the students I have taught over the last twelve years I would like to say a big 'thank you' for your many indirect contributions to this book.

First published by
Quilters Haven Publications in 2001

Reprinted 2002

Copyright © Karin Hellaby 2001

Graphics by Rosemary Muntus

Layout by Allan Scott

Photography by James Austen

Printed by EAM Printers,
Greenwich Business Park, Ipswich, Suffolk

ISBN 0-9540928-0-5   UPC 7 44674 0552 0

Quilters Haven Publications
68 High Street, Wickham Market
Suffolk, UK
IP13 0QU

Tel: +44 (0)1728 746275 Fax: +44 (0)1394 610525

www.quilters-haven.co.uk

Sew a Row Quilts
Karin Hellaby

Hearts a-glowing *by Karin Hellaby (19"x 16")*

Front cover: What if? *by Claire Frew (49"x 68")*

Page 1: Amish Rows *by Tricia Thornton (50" x 72")*

Page 3 (and back cover): Secret Rows *by Jan Allen (40"x 56")*

Back cover: Deben Rows *by Kathleen Brennan (23"x 31")*

Chapter guide

Introduction

Many of the Victorian cross stitch samplers are sewn in rows, which gave me the idea for a new teaching course – and this book.

The patchwork techniques used in *Sew a Row Quilts* are quick, simple and accurate. I have used the methods in classes for the past decade and students have found them fun and often magical. If you are short of time but have always wanted to make a quilt then this is the book for you!

Using my magic formula you have the freedom to pick out any of the techniques and sew various rows of patchwork. The choice of block size and technique for each row will individualise your quilt. The choice of fabric, patchwork and borders will give your quilt its own unique identity. Don't be frightened – working through the techniques included in this book will give you the confidence to experiment!

Don't like rows? Then use *Sew a Row Quilts* as a resource book to bring your knowledge of patchwork into the 21st century, using the latest methods, fabrics and equipment. Choose one patchwork technique and simply sew repeated blocks, still using the magic formula until you have a quilt top. Or try using two different techniques in alternating blocks, again using the formula, sewing into rows and joining the rows to make a quilt top.

Make the quilt any size you want! I have given guidelines for you to make a crib/ wall hanging, lap, single and double quilts.

Turning the patchwork top into a quilt can be a nightmare for beginner students and I have simplified this process. The rows can be sewn together horizontally or vertically using a stitch and flip technique incorporating the wadding and backing. This helps to stabilise the top ready for further quilting (if required).

Years ago quilts had a very practical use – they were often desperately needed for warmth, and fine hand quilting was a luxury. Instead several utilitarian hand stitching methods were used, some of which are included in this book. I feel they are a good alternative for those who want that quilt top finished as a quilt 'yesterday'.

I hope you will enjoy reading and working through this book as much as I have enjoyed writing it!

Early Sew a Row – designs taken from a 17th-century sampler

Using this book

Sew a Row Quilts is based on patchwork blocks that are sewn into rows. The rows are then sewn together into a quilt top. A simple 'magic formula' gives you the block sizes, and a structure for assembling a quilt top. Just choose a quilt size that you want to make – and start small, knowing you have the freedom to increase the size at any time.

The rows can be arranged either horizontally or vertically. You can use sashing (one fabric strip) to separate the rows, or not. The rows can all be different, or not. You can add outside borders, or not. You can finish with a lot of quilting, or not. The beauty of this formula is that it allows you the freedom of choice to make what you want – and the structure you need to be confident that you will create a really worthwhile result.

It isn't possible to estimate just how much fabric you will need for the quilt top. I suggest starting off with quarter metre/yard pieces of several fabrics (for a small quilt) and half metre/yard pieces for a larger quilt. If you have a favourite fabric, buy longer lengths of it. On the other hand, I often find that a quilt is more interesting if you run out of one fabric and have to find another!

Sew a Row patchwork is based on techniques I have used in classes over the last twelve years. They are simple. They are quick. They are efficient, both with fabric and with your time, and they will bring you up to date with the latest quiltmaking ideas. What's more, you'll find that you really do have time to make a quilt! Simply by working through the technique chapters that follow, you'll be able to create really satisfying results – and finally start using some of that wonderful fabric out there!

The chapters on technique are the main part of the book, and we've set them out with as few words as possible. The graphics at the side of the page will help you to identify each technique instantly. Many of us are visual learners, and I certainly find it tedious if I have to read a lot to learn the technique. When I work through written instructions I find that my eyes start to wander, and I waste time trying to find the place I have got to. I find it useful to clip a piece of plain paper to the page and slide it down to the point I've reached – not very sophisticated, perhaps, but it works for me and it might help you!

If you're a complete beginner then it really is worth starting at the beginning: the techniques become progressively more difficult as you work through the book. If you are already an experienced patch-worker, then dip in anywhere that takes your fancy. Once you have made enough blocks, turn to the final chapter to find out how to finish the quilt. And finally, if you prefer to work on a set project, we've provided block diagrams for several of the quilts featured on these pages, all ready for you to follow.

This is *your* resource book: I hope you'll enjoy it, and above all I hope you'll *have fun!*

Sew a Row
The Magic Quilt Formula

The magic number is **four**. It helps to know your four times table, as the rows are made from 4″ and 8″ blocks.

You can sew as many rows as you wish, and add sashings between one and two inches wide to separate the rows. The *width* of the rows will vary according to the size of quilt you are making, as shown in the **Sew a Row sizes** table below.

The way the formula works is that for a wall hanging a row could be six 4″ blocks or three 8″ blocks = 24″.

A single quilt could have a row with twelve 4″ blocks or six 8″ blocks = 48″.

You may add borders when all the rows are sewn together, to finish off the quilt neatly, or to make it slightly larger.

Sew a Row sizes...

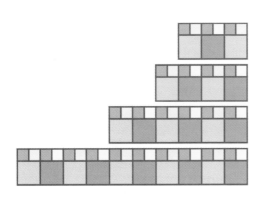

4″ and 8″ block counts

Blocks in a row – at a glance

	4″	8″	width
Crib / Wall hanging	6	3	24″
Lap quilt / quillow	8	4	32″
Single quilt	12	6	48″
Double quilt	20	10	80″

The quilt length can vary but I have suggested some standard lengths.

Crib / Wall hanging	28″
Lap quilt	56″
Single quilt	80″
Double quilt	80″

Wall hanging row variations

For example, the wall hanging could have seven 4″ high rows (= 28″), or three 4″ rows and two 8″ rows (= 28″). And the single quilt could have four 4″ rows and eight 8″ rows (= 80″), or eight 4″ rows and six 8″ rows (= 80″).

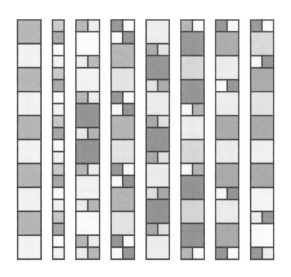

Some possible double quilt row combinations – there are many, many more!

If you want to separate the rows with sashing you will need to eliminate one or two rows of blocks. If you don't, the quilt may be too long (if you're making horizontal rows) or too wide (if you're making vertical rows).

This formula can also be used to work out the number of blocks needed for a quilt in which all the blocks are the same. A single quilt using an 8″ repeated block design would need 60 blocks (6 blocks in each of 10 rows).

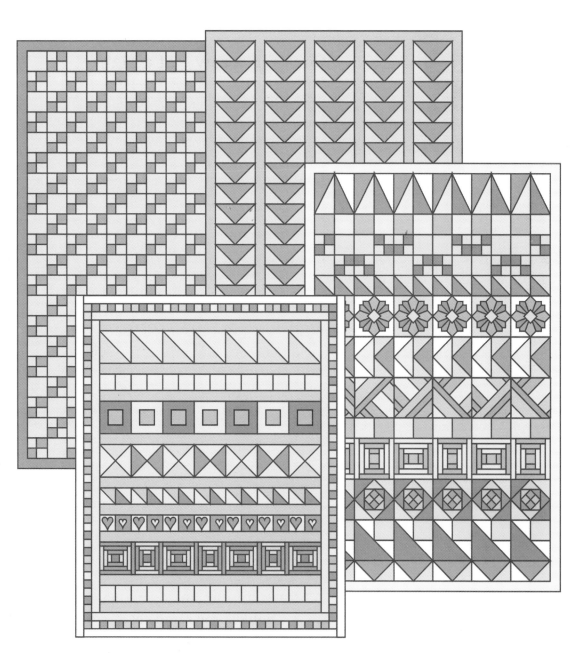

What do I need?

A guide to essential and not-so-essential equipment

Good tools are an investment that help you to enjoy your craft and achieve great looking quilts. The following list looks a little daunting. Only the essentials are essential. The others are tools that I mention in this book and I have therefore given you descriptions to help you decide if they would be useful to you.

Essentials

Sewing machine: make friends with your machine. Get to know it well, as you could be using it a lot in this book. Read through your instruction book and practice straight stitching. If you don't want to waste fabric then practice following lines on paper with your machine unthreaded. When I taught in schools I got the children to practice machine stitching straight lines, corners and curves drawn on paper.

I find a ¼" seam foot essential. If you haven't got one, you can mark the bed of the sewing machine with masking tape or buy an 'angler tool' to give you the necessary guidelines.

A walking foot, an open-toed embroidery foot and a darning foot are all useful but not essential.

Rotary cutting set (1 on photo opposite): i.e. a mat, ruler and cutter. Most of the instructions in this book have been written for rotary cutting, as it is faster and more accurate than using scissors. I use Omnigrid mats and rulers. The grid on the mat is accurate and only printed on the green side. I mostly use the unprinted grey side when I am using the ruler as my measurement guide as I don't need two sets of lines. The mat lasts longer if you use both sides. I use rulers and mats from the same manufacturer as the grids match accurately.

Buy the medium size mat 18" x 24", as with this size a normal width cotton fabric, folded once, fits comfortably. Start with a 6"x 24" Omnigrid ruler, as this size covers the folded fabric. The markings are visible on both light and dark fabrics.

A rotary cutter cuts through multiple layers of fabric in a single cut leaving a clean finished edge. Choose a medium or large size with good safety features and comfortable handle. I have always used an Olfa cutter, but recently I have started to use the Dritz 45mm pressure sensitive rotary cutter as it feels very comfortable in my hand and I don't have to remember to put on the safety guard every time I cut.

Iron: consider using a travel iron, as it is lighter and has no steam holes which can catch the fabric. Many prefer a heavy iron as it 'presses' better. Keep a water spray bottle close by to help with stubborn creases. Steam is rarely required in patchwork and can distort your work.

A small ironing board near your machine is ideal unless you want to lose weight; if so, put it at the far end of the house!

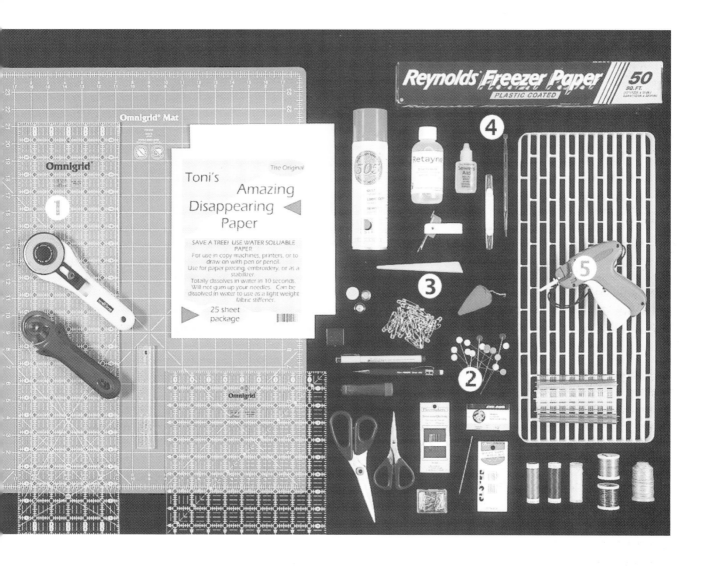

Thread: the rule is cotton thread for cotton fabric. Avoid the stronger polyester threads which can damage the fabric, and can melt when ironed on a cotton setting. I like Mettler and Gutterman 100% cotton threads. Mettler no. 60 is especially good for hand sewing – it threads easily and doesn't twist or knot when you're stitching.

Scissors: a small pair for snipping threads and appliqué; a larger pair for cutting fabric. Both must be able to cut precisely to the point. I like the Clover range, and use their patchwork scissors; they have a serrated edge which helps to 'hold' the fabric, and small cutwork scissors with a leather sheath to protect the blades. I also like the Gingher range of scissors.

Machine needles: need to be replaced after 6–8 hours of sewing!

● Size 70/10 or 80/12 for general sewing.

● Size 90/14 for foundation piecing as the needle is larger and makes bigger holes in the paper (making it easier to tear away later) Also use with heavier weight threads (like YLI Jeans thread) when machine quilting a bold line.

Quilting needles: more expensive, but some quilters prefer to use them all the time. These needles have a special taper to the point which prevents damage to fabric, and the eye is coated in Teflon to decrease the friction of the thread.

Metallica needles: these are designed for use with metallic threads, which you may wish to use for appliqué and machine quilting. The larger eye allows the thread to glide through without catching and breaking.

Hand sewing needles: different needles help with different types of sewing.

Hand appliqué: Sharps size 10 or 12 or Clover Gold Eye size 10 or 12, or Straws.

Hand quilting: Piecemaker betweens size 10.

Hand basting/tacking: Straw needles are great because they are long and very slender.

Utility tying/quilting: needles with larger eyes are needed to thread the thicker yarn. I suggest long doll needles or embroidery needles.

Pins: flower head pins **(2)** are 2″ long, fine and very sharp: ideal for pinning seams together when machine stitching. The flower heads lie flat so a ruler can be placed on top without distortion.

¾″ fine appliqué pins – small enough for appliqué and the smallest I feel comfortable handling. Some quilters use ½″ pins but I find them difficult to handle.

Mechanical propelling pencil: for greater accuracy when tracing and marking lines.

Freezer paper: made by Reynolds in America, this paper was originally used to wrap food for storing in the freezer. It comes on a roll in a box and can be purchased in supermarkets in America. In the UK quilt shops sell it by the metre. Buy a box when you can! Freezer paper has a matt/paper side and a shiny side. The paper side is for drawing on and tracing designs. Use a pencil only. The shiny side can be temporarily bonded to fabric by ironing. Test to make sure you can always remove it from the fabric, and bear in mind that it can be used several times without losing its bond and without leaving a residue. Quilters have found all sorts of uses for freezer paper. It is ideal for templates and used throughout this book.

If you can't get hold of freezer paper then try the wrappers from photocopying paper. I find them heavier and less flexible, but they are free if you make friends with your local copy shop.

Useful but not essential

These are the other tools that are in my sewing box and which I used when sewing samples for this book. In most cases you will only have to buy once so consider them an investment.

Add-a-quarter ruler has a lip which hinges to a template or folded fabric and, when you rotary cut, adds a ¼″ seam allowance. I like the 6″ length and find it ideal for foundation piecing and rotary cutting accurate shapes.

Chaco-liner: used to draw fine temporary chalk lines. The unit contains powdered chalk which is released when the wheel at the base rotates. Available in blue, pink, yellow and white.

Eraser: essential if you make mistakes when tracing.

Fray Check: a clear glue that can be used to prevent fraying in tight V shapes when hand appliquéing. Also great for reinforcing buttons on shirts, essential when you have three sons!

Little Wooden Iron (3) is about 4″ long and angled so that a minimum of pressure will give a good crease. I consider this essential, as finger pressing can lead to arthritis in the joints. Great for foundation piecing where a gentle press is required. Available for left and right handers. Not recommended for ironing shirts! Ideal when patchworking on trains and planes.

Needle threader for those of us who need help with threading needles. I recommend the Clover double needle threader which has one end for small eyed needles and the other for large.

Omnigrid Squares: the 9½″ size is particularly useful for cutting individual squares and rectangles, and for checking and trimming to final block sizes.

Pigma Pen: used for signing quilts. Pigma ink is permanent and washable. I also use it for naming my children's school uniform. Available in a variety of colours which will not 'spread' when applied.

Purple Thang (4): when I refer to this tool in classes it leads to all sorts of comments! It's a purple plastic stick with shaped ends that help you to push and poke without damaging the fabric.

505 Temporary Spray Adhesive can be used for quilt tacking and appliqué, as it will temporarily 'hold' everything together. Does not gum the needle and disappears leaving no residue. However, we have no idea what effect it will have on the quilt long term. Other similar products are available but this is the one that I use.

Thread Heaven: a new thread conditioner which works better than beeswax. I use it when hand sewing to prevent the thread from fraying and tangling.

Sewer's Aid: apply sparingly to the spool and bobbin threads to lubricate the thread as it passes through the machine. I use it for machine appliqué and any other decorative machine stitching.

Safety pins: I use 1″ solid brass gilt safety pins which do not rust and have sharp polished points for fastening the quilt layers before quilting. If you suffer from arthritis try the curved safety pins, as they are easier to insert and close.

Seam ripper for those few occasions when you need to unpick! I like a folding seam ripper as there is no cap to lose. When the blade dulls buy another ripper as there is a danger you can slip and cut the fabric instead of the thread.

Shirt tailor interfacing is a light iron-on vilene that I like to use as a template on top of fabric when sewing hand appliqué. It is soft to handle, stays on during sewing and yet peels off easily without leaving any residue. Always test first on spare fabric.

Spray starch fabrics to give them more body particularly after washing and to flatten fabric before rotary cutting. I buy the starch in an aerosol can and shake it well before using. Spray finely over the fabric, let it soak in and then iron the fabric for a crisp finish.

Try it first – as not everybody likes it – and be sure to use it in a well ventilated room.

Strawberry Emery: used to sharpen needles and pins so they last longer.

Thimbles: I consider these essential but not everybody likes to use them. I started using them when I suffered from a septic finger after changing nappies. Yes, those pinpricks can become infected, so persevere. The thimble should fit tightly, and there are a large range of different types, so there really is no excuse not to find one that will feel comfortable. Thimble-Its, a self-adhesive finger pad, are a popular alternative.

Toni's Water Soluble paper totally dissolves in water in about 10 seconds. I highly recommend this product for paper piecing foundations. It has always irritated me that I have had to resort to tweezers to remove paper from the back of foundations. Now all I need to do is 'swish' the finished foundation block in water to get rid of the paper. Can be drawn on, and used in ink or bubble jet printers and photocopying machines.

Quiltak System (5): used to tack the quilt layers together. A gun 'shoots' plastic tacks through the layers to temporarily hold the layers until they are quilted. A grid is needed to protect the work surface and the needle in the gun.

Retayne: a chemical solution that can seal the dye in commercial fabrics that are bleeding dye.

How to rotary cut

Rotary cutting has revolutionised patchwork as we can cut layers of fabric into strips and shapes without marking the fabric. This is quick and accurate. The rotary cutting set is made up of a mat, ruler and cutter. The cutter is a circular blade – very effective, and dangerous if not used correctly. Practise cutting paper instead of fabric until you feel confident. Confidence with rotary cutting only requires practice.

To cut strips of fabric

1 Iron the fabric along the warp and weft threads. Avoid ironing diagonally as you may stretch the fabric on the bias. Fold fabric in half, selvedges together, with a good, strong crease along the fold. If you have no selvedges, iron with the fold along the straight of the grain.

2 Place fabric on unmarked side of rotary cutting mat, folded edge nearest you. Lay ruler on top, matching a horizontal line of the ruler to the fabric fold.

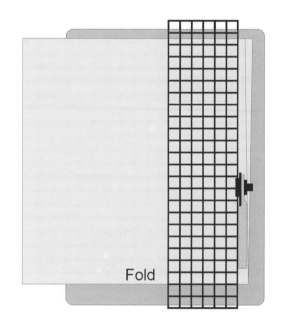

3 Rotary cut against the right side of the ruler (left handers rotary cut on the left). Remove safety cover on the cutter and lean the cutter against the ruler; hold it firmly, pushing it down with your index finger. Start cutting before crossing the bottom fold, pushing away from you. Halfway up the side, stop cutting, leaving the cutting hand in position, and move your other hand along the ruler to steady it before continuing the cut. If you find the ruler wobbles, spread your fingers so the small finger rests on the fabric. As a last resort, you can attach fabric grippers to your ruler. (I dislike them because they make it impossible to slide the ruler.) Always cut away from you, and when you complete the cut, **replace the safety guard.** This first cut straightens the edge of the fabric.

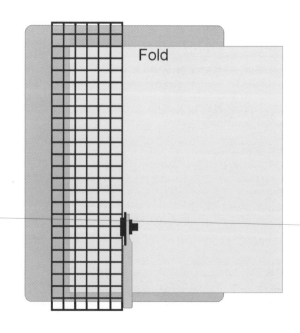

4 Turn the mat through 180°, or walk to the opposite side of the board. The straight edge you have cut will now be on your left.

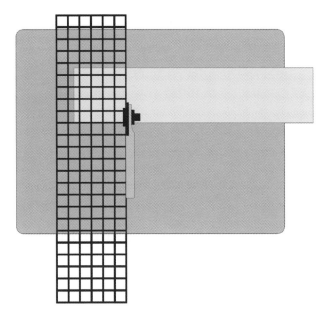

5 You are now ready to cut fabric strips. Place the ruler so the exact width measurement you need is precisely aligned to the newly cut edge of the fabric, ensuring the fold is still lined up with one of the horizontal guidelines. Rotary cut as before.

Multiple squares from strips

Using 4½″ squares as an example:

1 Place a pre-cut 4½″ fabric strip on the mat. This will be cut while still folded.

2 Square up the strip selvage end, removing the selvage completely.

3 Turn the mat through 180°.

4 Lay the ruler on the fabric so that the 4½″ mark lines up with the newly cut edge, and the top of the fabric is in line with a ruler line. Rotary cut. Each cut will give you two squares.

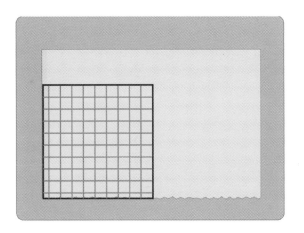

Cutting one square

Using an 8½″ square as an example:

1 Place a 9½″ square ruler in the bottom left-hand corner of the fabric. Trim away excess fabric on the right and top.

2 Remove the ruler, and rotate the fabric square through 180°.

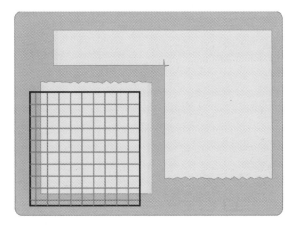

3 Place the 8½″ ruler lines on the newly cut edges.

4 Trim off excess fabric to the right and along the top.

How to select fabric

100% dress weight cotton is recommended for patchwork as it handles well and can generally be manipulated to do what is required. 100% raw silk is fine to use once you have some experience of the techniques. If using silk, you may wish to stabilise it with a light iron-on vilene. Silk and cotton can be used together as long as the weights are similar.

Work with the best quality fabrics available from your local quilt store. All the time and effort you spend making a quilt could be in vain if the fabric stretches and distorts as you are cutting and sewing. Bargain fabrics are often the ones that are improperly processed, have fewer threads to the inch or lose excessive dye during washing.

Choosing fabric for a quilt can be intimidating for a beginner quilter and sometimes even for those who have experience. If you are new to this craft then try to find a good quilt shop whose staff have years of quilting experience behind them, and ask for help.

This is one of the methods I use to help new customers.

1 Choose a main fabric that you love and can't live without. This should be a print fabric with more than one colour.

2 Look carefully at the chosen print and pick out the colour(s) you want to emphasise.

3 Now try to find light, medium and dark value fabrics in these colours. The value of a fabric changes with the companion fabric that is placed next to it. It is this *contrast* that is most important in patchwork, otherwise all the shapes merge.

4 Vary the scale of prints for more interest. Think about using small and large scale prints, stripes, plaids all of which can give a varied texture to your patchwork.

5 If you have chosen several colour groups, look for 'bridging' fabrics that combine at least two of the colours. These fabrics ease the transition from one colour to the next.

Once you have chosen, stand back and look at the fabrics from a distance. Do they look good together? If not, add more or substitute others.

The more you 'play' with fabrics the more confident you will become. The only rule is contrast; all others are guidelines which I have seen broken over and over again with some wonderful results. Learn to rely on your own gut feeling about colour and fabric – if you like it you will make it work, and you are more likely to enjoy making the quilt.

Study quilts that you like, and look carefully at the fabric combinations that have been chosen.

Choose a fabric that really appeals and try to match colours from it.

The quilts featured in this book show many different ways of choosing fabric:

- Use solid/plain fabrics only.

- Choose a theme such as Stars and Stripes, Christmas, Brights, Country or Baby.

- Introduce black and white prints to make other colours sparkle.

- Make backgrounds interesting by using several neutrals instead of one.

- Let a striped border print become the main focus of the quilt.

Washing fabric

Pre-wash the fabric just in case there is any excess dye and shrinkage. Divide the fabric into separate colour groups and soak in warm water, there is no need to add a detergent. Rinse. Dry in the dryer or out of direct sunlight. Iron whilst still damp, taking care not to stretch the fabric along the bias. If you like the stiffness of new fabric then spray starch and iron.

If there is dye loss after rinsing, add a solution of one part white vinegar to two parts water as a final rinse or use 'Retayne' solution to seal the dye.

How much do I need to buy?

Unless you are only using one or two blocks and repeating them throughout the quilt then this is a difficult question to answer. Few quilters like to plan everything on paper in advance and then stick to their plan.

I prefer to collect some fabrics together and just start sewing, arranging the patchwork blocks once I have a few sewn. If this is going to be your approach then buy a selection of quarter yards/metres for a small project and buy halves or one yard/metre lengths for larger projects. If you run out and can't get any more this is not a disaster. Choose a similar fabric and your quilt will still look good! After all, this is patchwork!

Some information on the additional Quilt Layers

Wadding

This is the layer that goes between the patchwork top and fabric backing. There are many waddings available ranging from polyesters, cotton, cotton blends, wool and silk. If possible, try out a small piece of wadding first before committing yourself to a bed size piece. Good quilting shops will sell smaller sample squares of their different waddings, ideal for you to try in a small project. The newer firm waddings such as cotton, cotton mixes and needled polyesters are ideal for the sew and flip method of layering and quilting in one go.

If a wadding feels like a pan scrub, which is sometimes the case with English polyester waddings, then be wary – they could wear your quilt from the inside out!

Quilt backing

Traditionally the third and final layer is 100% cotton fabric. A new alternative is to use fleece polyester: this is a thick piled fabric, great for backing a patchwork top – and you can forget the wadding. You get a warm cuddly patchwork coverlet or rug which is not technically a quilt, as it only has two layers instead of three.

Sewing Tips

Unless you are told otherwise, always sew your seams with a scant ¼" seam allowance (i.e. one or two threads less than ¼"). This is more accurate than an exact ¼" because a small amount of fabric is lost due to the thickness of the thread and the bulk created by pressing the seam allowances in one direction. Try the seam allowance test in Strip a Row Chequer board (p.20).

Sew straight stitches with a slightly smaller than medium stitch; no tying off is needed unless indicated. The stitching should be small enough not to come undone, but large enough to 'unpick' if you go wrong.

Use a neutral colour thread (cream, beige, or grey) so you don't need to change thread colour when you change fabrics.

Sew from cut edge to cut edge. If your machine does not like doing this, then start sewing on a folded scrap of fabric, sew onward into the adjacent patchwork, and finish sewing on to a second adjacent fabric scrap. This will help prevent the first and last stitches distorting.

Chain piecing speeds up sewing. Feed the patchwork pieces through the sewing machine without cutting the threads between them. Your pieces will look like a line of washing. When you have finished, cut them apart by snipping through the chained thread joining the pieces.

Pin at right angles to the seams; that way the seams don't move, and it's easy to slip the pins out as you stitch towards them. I use fine flower pins.

When matching two pieces of patchwork, I pin the seams at each end and then evenly along the length. If one piece is slightly longer, pin the fabric first (matching each end) and sew with the excess side down.

Miraculously, the extra fabric seems to disappear!

When sewing small pieces of patchwork, pins are unnecessary; use the abutting seam technique (see p.20) for perfect seam matching. Lay the pieces right sides together with seams pressed in opposite directions so that they fit together. With the top seam opposing the seam direction, the two seams will nestle and wrestle for a perfect match.

Use a flower pin to guide the fabric towards the needle. Using the tip of your finger can be dangerous as it could disappear under the needle.

A 'needle-stop down' position is a great asset. If your machine has one, do use it.

Fit a new machine needle every 6–8 hours of sewing. A blunt needle damages the fabric and causes uneven stitching.

Many people confuse ironing and pressing. Ironing is a back and forth sweeping motion that is used on clothes and fabrics to remove wrinkles. In quiltmaking we mostly press; which is the gentle lowering, pressing and lifting of the iron along seams. Perfectly cut and sewn patchwork can become distorted by excessive ironing.

Setting seam stitches is a technique I frequently use as it helps to bed the stitches into the fabric. After sewing a seam I press the seam and then open up the patch and gently press it in one direction towards the darker fabric. If this is too bulky then press the seam open. Often I 'finger' press with a little wooden iron as there is less distortion.

Sewing small, straight **stay stitches** close to the fabric edge helps to stabilise the fabric and stop it stretching – a good technique to use before adding borders or binding.

Strip a Row

Sewing strips of fabric together gives you exciting and versatile patchwork. It also 'grows' quickly, giving you fast results.

I like to use crisp, firm cotton fabric for the strips. I often spray starch the fabric to give it a firm flatness before cutting.

To make sure you are cutting and sewing accurately, try the chequer board sample first. By joining several chequer board pieces you can make a simple but effective row for your quilt.

Chequer Board

1. Cut two 2½" strips from the width of fabric, one in dark and one in light fabric.

2. Stitch along the length using a ¼" seam.

3. Press along the seam to bed the stitches.

4. From the front, sweep the side of the iron from light to dark fabric, making sure no folds occur at the seam when pressing. Fold strip in half across the width and press a crease line.

5. Cut the strip in half on the crease line and fit right sides together, reversing the light and dark fabrics so that the seams nestle against one another.

6. Rotary cut to straighten one end at right angles to the seam. Cut off at least four pairs of 2½" pieces.

7. Stitch together, opposing the seam and making the pairs nestle and wrestle for a perfect match. Use a flower pin to guide the fabric towards the needle, and chain stitch each pair, one after the other.

8. Take two of these fours, and sew them together to make a rectangle consisting of eight squares. This is your test piece.

9. Press on the reverse side, by sweeping the iron from one side while slightly pulling the patchwork with your other hand.

10. The finished piece should measure exactly 4½"x 8½". Adjust the seam if the sample is too large or too small, and sew another test piece if necessary.

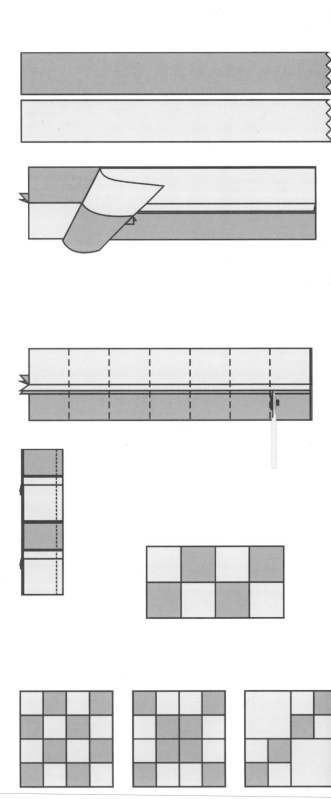

QH Tip

Use a smaller than medium stitch when sewing together strips of fabric that will be re-cut to make patchwork. A larger stitch could unravel before you finish stitching.

Detail (top) from Silken Climbers *by Anne Smith (see p.110) , with chequer board used to frame an appliqué strip, and* Roman Tile *(33"x 50") by Clare Dunderdale, using chequer board as a main theme.*

21

Chop Suey Strips

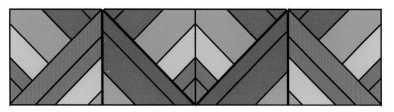

Cutting instructions

4" block

Cut a strip the width of the fabric from each of six or more fabrics, varying the widths. When sewn together the resulting strip set must be 7" wide (e.g. 1", 1¼", 1½", 1¾", 1¾", 2½" will be slightly wider, ready for trimming to size).

8" block

Cut a strip the width of the fabric from each of nine or more fabrics, varying the widths. When sewn together the resulting strip set should be 12½" wide (e.g. 1¼", 1¼", 1½", 1¾", 1¾", 2", 2", 2½", 3½" will be slightly wider, ready for trimming to size).

1 Arrange your strips, noting that the outside strips will dominate in this design.

2 Sew together with a scant ¼" seam, reversing the stitching direction when adding each strip. If you sew strips all in one direction, the strip set may develop a curve.

3 Press all seams in one direction.

4 Check width measurement and trim if necessary to the required 7" or 12½" width.

5 Cut the strip set into squares (either 7" wide or 12½" wide).

 When travelling around Norway eleven years ago, I saw a patchwork cushion that would make an interesting quilt design. From then on, 'chop suey' became a favourite with my students.

 A set of contrasting fabric strips are sewn together and then chopped up to create interesting designs.

QH Tip

Instead of getting involved in complicated maths, plan to make the strip set slightly wider – then you can cut it down to the correct width.

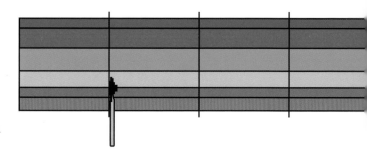

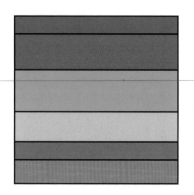

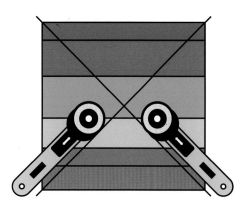

6 Cut each square twice diagonally from corner to corner to make four triangles.

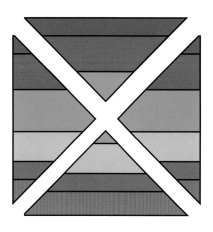

7 Try arranging the triangles in different ways until you find a design you like. You will need to sew two triangles together to form a block. Press this seam open, otherwise there will be a lot of bulk.

8 Sew the squares together into a row for your quilt.

QH Tip

Create another lovely Chop Suey design by stitching two rows together. You can see the results in many of the quilts in this book, including the example on the right, a detail from *Amish Rows* by Tricia Thornton (see p.1 for the full quilt).

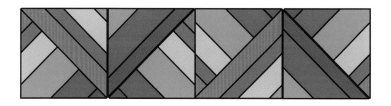

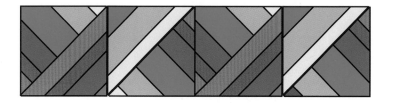

Roman Stripes

Cutting instructions

(measurements are oversized, so that the finished band can be trimmed to the correct size if necessary)

 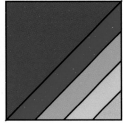

Two complementary blocks are created from this technique.

4" blocks

Background – cut a 3½" strip, width of fabric

4 strips – cut one of each – 1¼", 1¼", 1¼", and 1½", width of fabric

8" blocks

Background – cut a 6¼" strip, width of fabric

5 strips – cut one of each – 1¼", 1½", 1¾", 2", and 2", width of fabric

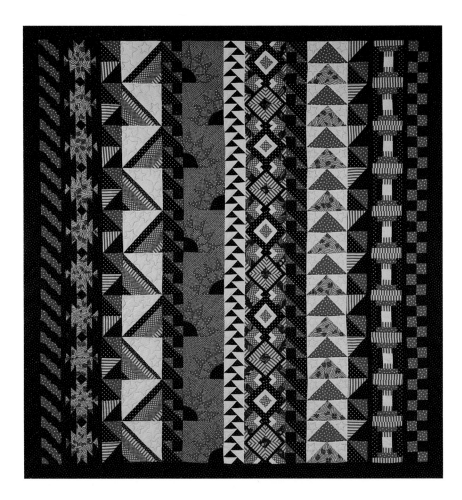

Stars and Stripes *(above, 87"x 90") by Heather Langdon, uses Roman Stripes in the fourth strip from the left – while Jan Allen's quilt* Secret Rows *(detail below – full quilt on p.3) also makes very good use of this technique.*

24

1 Sew the strips together, reversing direction of stitching when adding each strip, until you have completed a strip set. If you sew strips all in one direction a curve can develop in the strip set.

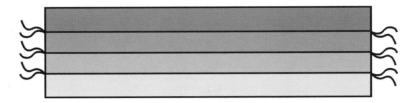

2 From the front gently press the seams in one direction.

3 Trim the strip set width to fit the background strip.

4 Place the strip set right sides together with the background and sew down both long sides. Press to bed the seams.

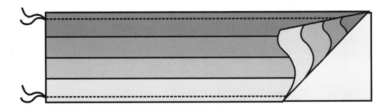

5 Use the 45° line on your ruler lined up to the edge of the fabric to make a cut diagonally across the strip set. Repeat in the opposite direction, to cut triangles. Using a right-angled triangle ruler makes these cuts easier.

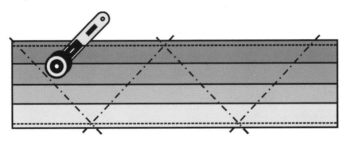

6 Gently pull out the small row of stitches at the top of the triangle, open out triangle to reveal a square. Press towards the strip set. Cut off 'ears'. Trim to the correct size if necessary.

7 Have fun arranging the blocks in your row!

Courthouse Steps

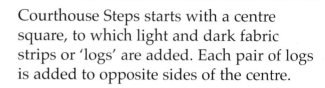

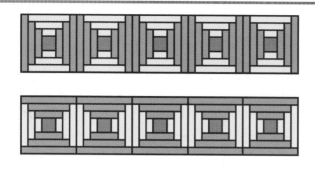

Courthouse Steps starts with a centre square, to which light and dark fabric strips or 'logs' are added. Each pair of logs is added to opposite sides of the centre.

I use a chain piecing method (see p. 18) where you sew and then cut. At each stage you take all the blocks you need for the row, add the next fabric, and then cut.

Cutting instructions

4" block

Centre dark square – cut 1½" strip, then cut 1¼" strips in dark and light fabrics.

8" block

Centre dark square – cut 2½" strip, then cut 1½" strips in dark and light fabrics.

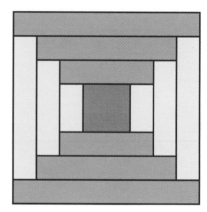

4" block (above) and 8" block (right)

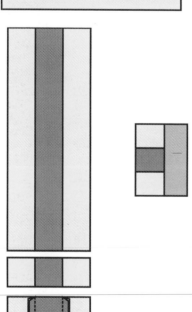

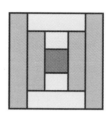

1 Sew light fabric strips to either side of centre fabric. Press to bed the stitches, then press outwards to light fabrics. Cut 1½"(4" block) or 2½" (8" block) pieces, one for each block.

2 Sew dark fabric strips to opposite sides of the centre section. It is faster and usually more accurate to chain piece all the blocks at the same time. Place a dark fabric strip right side up on the bed of the machine. Lower the presser foot and the needle into position on the ¼" seam mark. Lift the presser foot, leaving the needle in the fabric strip. Just in front of the needle, place the centre section right side down on the dark fabric, matching raw edges. Lower the presser foot and stitch into place with a scant ¼" seam. Finish sewing with your needle in the fabric just past the patchwork. Lift the presser foot and position the next centre section. Sew into position, and repeat until all centres have been sewn. Remove from the machine. Cut apart at

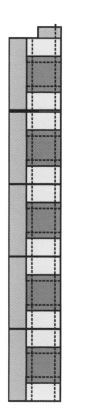

right angles to seam line, alongside raw edges. Press outwards from the centre.

3 Sew a dark fabric to the opposite side of the centre sections exactly as you did in step 2. Cut apart and again press away from the centre.

4 Continue in the same way, sewing a light fabric alongside the light section.

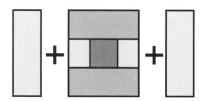

5 Continue adding light and dark fabrics until you have reached the correct size of either 4½″ or 8½″ (finished block with ¼″ seam allowances all round)

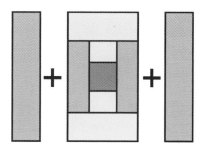

6 Arrange blocks as desired and sew into a row.

QH Tip

If your blocks turn out to be not quite big enough, make the last round of strips wider and then trim the block down to the size you need.

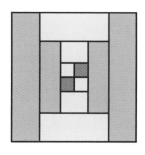

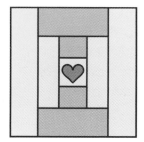

What if...

🔲 You started with a light fabric in the centre?

🔲 The centre square was a four patch?

🔲 You appliquéd onto the centre patch?

🔲 All the logs were different fabrics?

Greek Keys

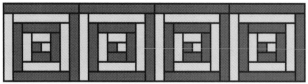

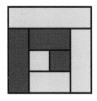

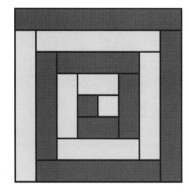

4" block (above) and 8" block (right)

 Greek Keys can be seen as a decoration on old buildings and patterns on mosaic floors.

 The strips are sewn from the centre out, but this time arranging the dark and light fabrics to look like a spiral. Keep spiralling until you reach the block size you need.

Cutting instructions

Cut 1½" strips in two contrasting fabrics.

1 Sew a light and dark strip together with a scant ¼" seam. To calculate the length of fabric required, multiply the number of blocks by 1½".

2 Press, to bed the stitches, and then press towards the dark fabric.

3 Cut the strip unit into 1½" pieces, one for each block you are making. It is quicker to fold the strip into a double layer and cut two at a time.

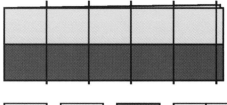

4 Add a light strip to one long side, and a dark strip to the opposite long side. All the blocks can be chain pieced using the method shown in Courthouse Steps (p.26).

5 Press the seams outwards. Trim pieces to 2½" x 3½".

6 Continue to add light and dark strips on opposite long sides until you reach your chosen block size (4½" or 8½"). Press well. Check size and trim if necessary.

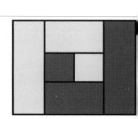

7 Arrange your key blocks in a row design
and sew together.

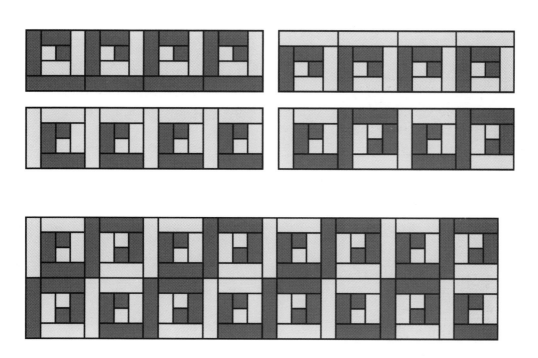

QH Tip

Choose the light or dark fabric to dominate in the Greek Key block by sewing one or the other as the final strip.

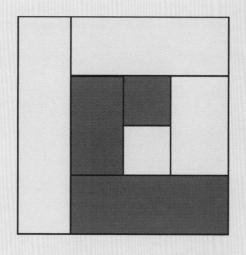

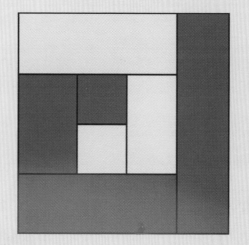

*Notice how light dominates in
the upper design, and dark in
the lower design.*

Triangle Magic

Why 'Triangle Magic'? Because there is an almost magical way to make triangles from squares and rectangles without the need to cut the triangles from templates, and without the need to sew nasty, stretchy bias seams. Triangles are very popular in patchwork: these variations give you an almost infinite choice, especially if you combine them with other Sew a Row blocks.

 Half square triangles – just a regular square divided into two triangles.

 Quarter square triangles – the same square, but this time divided by two diagonal lines. Now there are four triangles inside the square.

 Delectable Mountains – with a little extra work, you can modify your half square triangles to give a new way of creating this traditional pattern.

 Skinny triangle – this time a rectangle is divided into two triangles.

 Squared-up Triangles – this square ends up with a triangle in one half; the other half has two triangles and a smaller square.

Once you know the super quick methods for making these units you can have a lot of fun combining them into blocks for your Sew a Row. To tempt you to have a go, look at the rows below. Really exciting blocks can be created from these units!

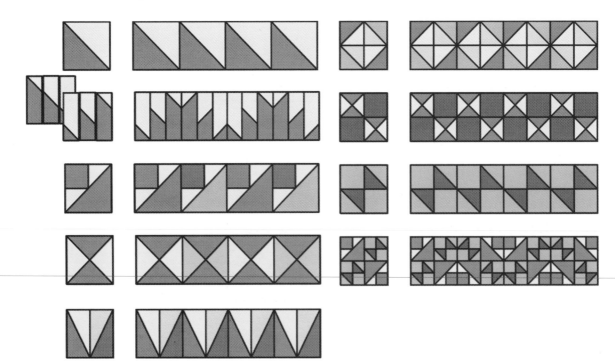

Half Square Triangles

Cutting instructions

Use two contrasting fabrics, iron right sides together, and spray starch if necessary to help them adhere. A strip width of fabric produces ten 4" blocks.

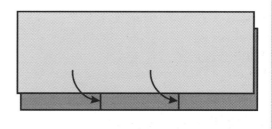

4" block: cut a $4^7/_8$" strip, cut the strip into $4^7/_8$" squares.

8" block: sew together four of the 4" finished units.

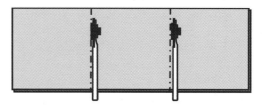

You should now have two matching contrasting squares. Keep them exactly together as they have been cut. Each pair of squares gives you two 4" blocks.

1 Proceed with the square kept together in their contrasting pairs. Mark a diagonal line on the wrong side of the lightest square.

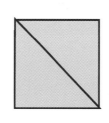

2 Stitch ¼" away from the marked line. Sew one side of the line, pull the unit away from the presser foot without breaking the thread and then sew down the other side again ¼" away from the line.

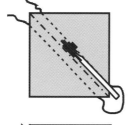

3 Press to bed the stitches.

4 Cut on the marked line to divide the square into two equal triangles.

5 Open the triangle to magically reveal a square with two contrasting triangles. Then open the other to reveal the same.

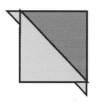

6 Gently press the centre seam towards the dark fabric. Take care not to stretch the seam whilst you are pressing.

7 Cut off the 'ears'.

Make more half square triangles and arrange then into a row or wait until you have tried other magic triangles which could make the row even more interesting!

Delectable Mountains

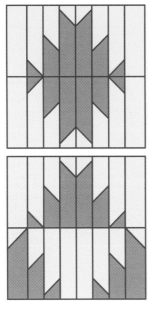
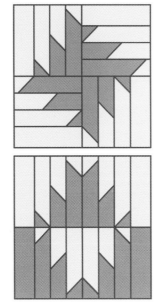

A block that looks like strips but starts with squares! There is no wasted fabric with these blocks, and those bias seams just happen. Read on to find out how!

Cutting instructions

Each pair of squares produces two blocks.

4" block

Cut $4^7/_8$" wide fabric from a light and dark fabric. Iron right sides together, cut into $4^7/_8$" squares.

8" block

Stitch four 4" completed blocks together.

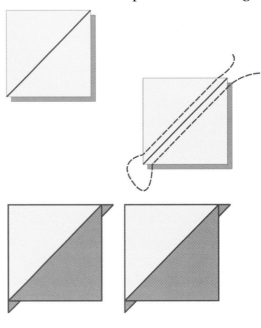

1 On the wrong side of the light square, mark a diagonal line from corner to corner.

2 Stitch a scant ¼" either side of the marked line. Press to set the stitches.

3 Cut on the marked line. Open up to reveal two half square triangles. Press the seams towards the dark fabric. Cut off 'ears'.

4 Layer the squares right sides together, colours opposing.

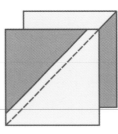

5 Cut three 1½" vertical strips.

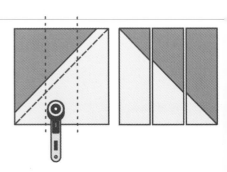

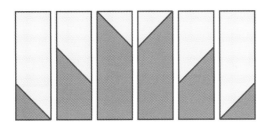

6 Arrange the strips as shown, choosing either a dark mountain with a light sky or a light mountain against a dark sky.

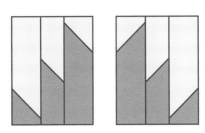

7 Sew strips together with a scant ¼" seam. From the wrong side press lightly in one direction. Turn right side up and iron, pulling the block to the correct width.

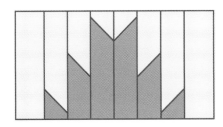

8 The blocks should now measure 4½" x 3½". To make the blocks square, stitch a 1½" strip of sky fabric to one side.

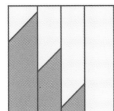

9 The blocks can be sewn together in various ways to make 4" high and 8" high rows.

What if...?

You re-arranged the strips to form 'creative' mountains?

You cut squares from different fabrics so that the mountains changed colour?

You cut squares from different fabrics and varied the strips in a block? This gives you multi-fabric mountains rather than one solid colour.

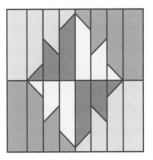

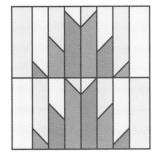

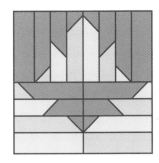

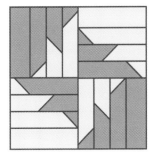

33

Quarter Square Triangles

Cutting instructions

Take two contrasting fabrics, iron right sides together, spray starch if necessary to help them adhere to one another. A strip width of fabric produces nine 4" blocks.

4" block: cut a 5¼" strip, cut the strip into 5¼" squares.

8" block: sew together four 4" quarter square triangles.

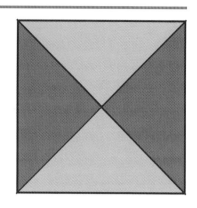

You now have two matching, contrasting squares. Keep them exactly together as they have been cut. Each pair of squares produces two 4" quarter square triangle blocks.

1 Follow steps 1–7 as in Half Square Triangles (see p.31).

see p.31

2 On the wrong side of one half square triangle mark a diagonal line which crosses over the seam line from corner to corner.

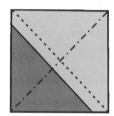

3 Place this square right sides together with an unmarked half square triangle, reversing the colours against one another. Nestle the centre seams and pin diagonally where they fit.

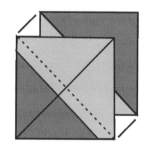

4 Starting from the direction where you will oppose the top centre seam (this will push it into the seam below for a perfect matching centre) sew either side of the marked line.

5 Press to bed the stitches.

6 Cut on the diagonal line. Open up two squares.

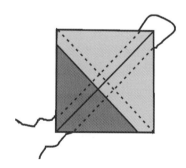

7 Gently press the seam in one direction, admiring your perfectly matched centre points.

What if...

You placed a plain square right sides together with a half square triangle?

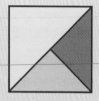

You wanted four different fabrics in your final square?

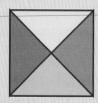

Skinny Triangles

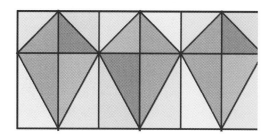

Cutting instructions

Skinny triangles are easy when sewn with a stable bias seam. Take two contrasting fabrics, iron right sides together, spray starch if necessary to help them adhere to one another.

4″ blocks: cut 2½″ strips. Cut strip into 4½″ rectangles (two units make one block).

8″ blocks: can be sewn from eight completed skinny triangles.

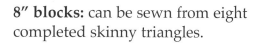

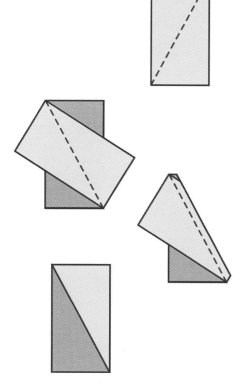

1. On the wrong side of the lightest rectangles draw a line diagonally from the lower left to the upper right corner.

2. Place one of the marked rectangles on top of a dark rectangle, right sides together. Position the rectangle so that the marked lines line up with the top left and bottom right corners of the unmarked rectangle.

3. Sew *on* the line.

4. Press to bed the stitches.

5. Cut away excess fabric ¼″ from the sewn line.

6. Gently press towards the dark fabric. Cut off ears.

7. Sew two pieced rectangles together with a scant ¼″ seam to make a 4″ block. The tip of the triangle will be ¼″–½″ below the raw edge in the finished block.

What if...

You marked the light rectangle from lower right to upper left? The opposite units sewn together would give you an isosceles triangle.

Squared-up Triangles

Cutting instructions

4" block

Cut a 2½" dark strip

Cut a 3½" light strip

Cut a 4½" dark strip, then cut into 5½" rectangles.

1   Sew the first two strips, 2½" and 3½" right sides together along their length with a scant ¼" seam.

2   Press to bed the seams. From the right side and using the side of the iron, press the seam towards the dark fabric. Fold strip in half lengthways and crease to mark halfway point.

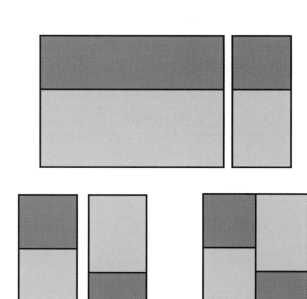

3   Cut strip in half, place right sides together reversing colours. Straighten one end, cut 2½" units, two at a time.

4   Sew pairs of these units as shown, matching the outside edges and chain piecing.

5   Clip the seam allowance to within a few threads of the seam line in the seam between the two squares.

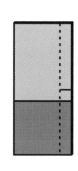

6   Press units from the wrong side, pressing seams away from the squares.

7   Using a ruler, on the wrong side of the unit, mark a line from a light corner and touching the inside dark square, as in the diagram. It is important that the line goes through the X of the seams. Repeat the same on the opposite side. There should now be two diagonal lines parallel to one another on the rectangle unit.

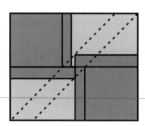

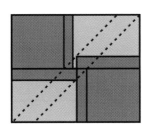 

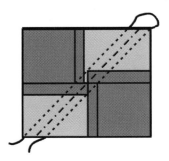

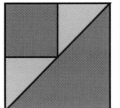 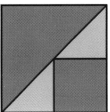

8 Place one of these pieced units right sides together with a 5½″ x 4½″ rectangle of dark fabric. Sew on each of the drawn lines. Press. Cut apart by cutting through between the seams. Open out to reveal two blocks.

If you have 'kites' try again looking carefully at the diagrams!

What if...

You reverse the light and dark fabrics?

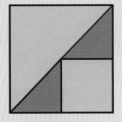

You have a half square triangle in the small square?

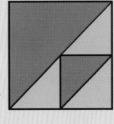

Fly with the Geese

Flying Geese are a traditional patchwork pattern seen on many quilts. As well as looking attractive in rows they are also frequently used as quilt borders.

The goose shape can be used as a roof on a house, the main part of a tree and in its migrating pattern as a shoal of fish. It's all in the fabric and placement. Use these wonderfully quick and accurate methods to sew a row, and let your imagination fly with the geese!

Not all patchwork geese need to be flat! Many find 3D geese (see next page) easier than the other two. They can be used in the same designs as the flying geese on pages 40–43.

Used with imagination, this technique can suggest many things besides geese – in What if? *(below and front cover) Claire Frew makes charming use of Flying Geese to suggest house roofs (above) and fish (below).*

A detail from Shades of the Orient *by Pat Boyes (above, full quilt on p.110) showing 3D geese 'in flight'.*

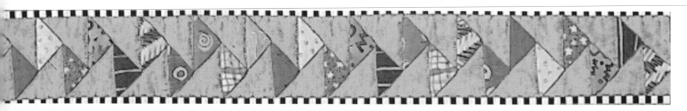

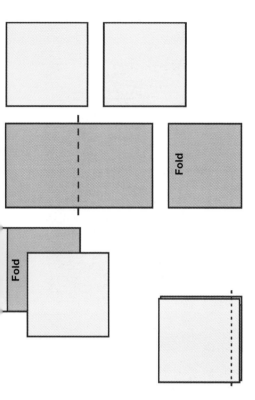

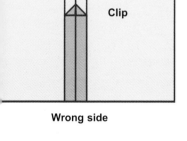

Wrong side

3D Geese

Cutting instructions (for one goose)

4″ finished width.

Background – cut two 2½″ squares.

Goose – cut one rectangle 4½″ x 2½″.

1 Fold the goose fabric rectangle in half, wrong sides together, pin. This unit should measure 2¼″ x 2½″.

2 Place the folded goose onto the right side of a background square, matching up the corners away from the fold. Pin.

3 Place the second square on top, right sides down so that the goose is the filling between the squares. Pin.

4 Sew along one side at right angles to the fold.

5 Press the goose open, making sure it is pressed evenly as it must look balanced from side to side. It helps to clip the tip of the goose seam so that it lies flat and open.

6 Stitch the geese together following instructions under 'flying geese'.

QH Tip

Stay stitch the base of the goose before sewing it together.

What if...

You sewed two geese together along their base? You would create a 3D square within a square...

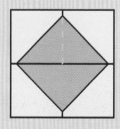

Flying Geese

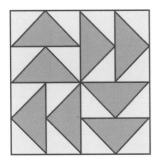

 With this quick method the geese will be flying along the row in no time!

 It eliminates the need to cut out all those triangles and stitch them together along stretchy bias edges.

 Another plus is that there is no wastage of fabric.

This is an adaptation of a method first shown to me by Pauline Adams.

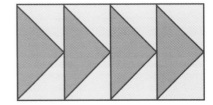

Four geese

Cutting instructions to make four geese

The basic block is made from two geese.

4" block

Cut 4 x 2⁷/₈" squares in background fabric; cut one 5¼" square in goose fabric

8" block

Cut 4 x 4⁷/₈" squares in background fabric; cut one 9¼" square in goose fabric. Alternatively the 8" block can be made from eight smaller geese!

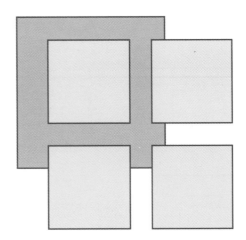

1 Place large goose square right side up and lay two small background squares exactly in opposite corners wrong side up.

2 Where they cross each other in the centre, trim the corners. Use a ruler to mark a straight line diagonally from corner to corner on the small squares. Pin.

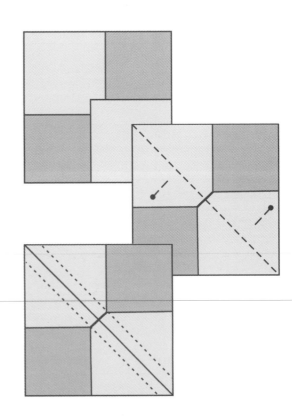

3 Machine stitch a scant ¼" seam on both sides of the diagonal line.

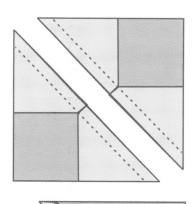

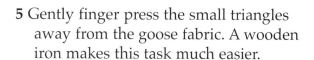

4 Cut apart on the centre line between the lines of stitching.

5 Gently finger press the small triangles away from the goose fabric. A wooden iron makes this task much easier.

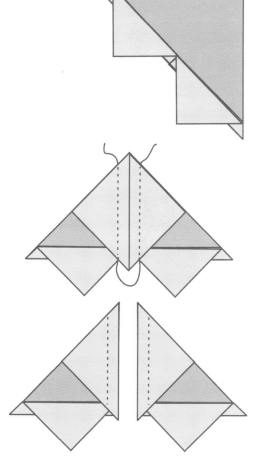

6 Draw a diagonal line on the wrong sides of the remaining small squares. With right sides together pin one into the 'empty' corner on the goose and stitch a ¼" seam on both sides of the marked line. Repeat with the remaining half section.

7 Cut apart on the marked line between the lines of stitching.

8 Press the four pieces carefully using the side of the iron to avoid distortion. The sky fabric is pressed away from the goose.

To sew together:

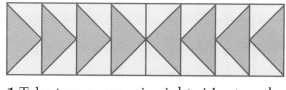

1 Take two geese, pin right sides together, placing pins at right angles to the seam. Pin at each end and in the centre.

2 Sew from the side where you can see the X (formed by the stitching) on the goose tip. Sew with a scant ¼" seam stitching through the centre of the X. Press away from the goose tip.

3 Continue stitching geese pairs together into your chosen design.

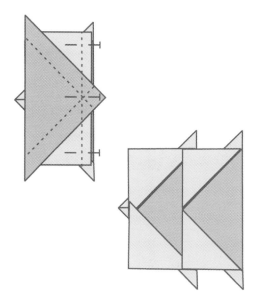

41

Migrating Geese

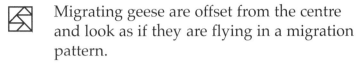 Migrating geese are offset from the centre and look as if they are flying in a migration pattern.

As you make the geese, half will fly on the left and the other half fly on the right.

The geese are then sewn together as a continuous skein flying across your quilt.

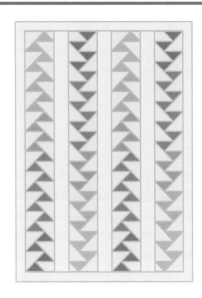

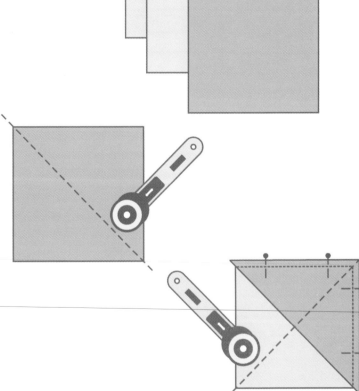

There are three geese in each block, although these quick instructions make four geese from each set of squares.

Cutting instructions to make four geese

4" finished width

Cut 2 x $3^5/_8$" squares in background fabric.
Cut one $3^7/_8$" square in goose fabric.

8" finished width

Cut 2 x $6^1/_4$" squares in background fabric.
Cut one $6^5/_8$" square in goose fabric.

1 Cut the goose square in half along one diagonal line.

2 Right sides together, lay one goose triangle in the corner of a background square. Mark a diagonal line from goose corner to background corner.

3 Stitch a scant ¼" seam around the two sides of the triangle, turning on the diagonal line by leaving the needle inserted and then lifting the presser foot before you turn.

4 Cut in half along the marked line to give one left and one right hand unit. Press towards the dark fabric. Cut off any 'ears'.

5 Lay out the units to form the design.

6 Take the lowest pair of units and stitch together. Press. Then add the next unit. Press. Continue sewing from the bottom up until the strip is completed.

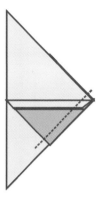

7 Trim the strip ¼″ below the marked line at short ends as shown.

8 Sew a trimmed background fabric triangle from the base of the strip to fill the gap next to the top goose.

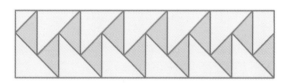

What if?

You mix various fabric geese along the row?

You mix graduated background fabrics along the row?

Down the Patchwork Path

Curved patchwork has always been thought of as 'advanced'. Using this technique it becomes fast, accurate and easy. Start with a circle applied to a square, then cut into four. Now you have four curved patchwork units which can be sewn into a block!

Just look at the many different blocks you could try as you take a circular path through the patchwork.

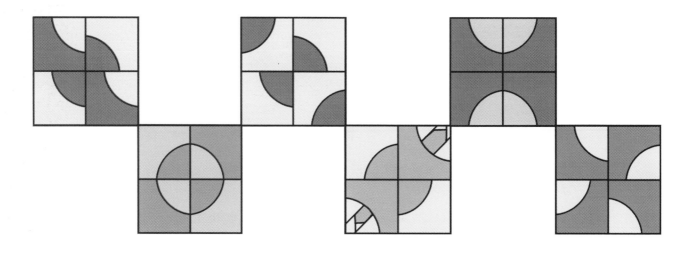

(Above) Four curved squares suitable for 4" or 8" blocks.

(Below) Sixteen curved squares suitable for 8" blocks – each square is 2" on each side.

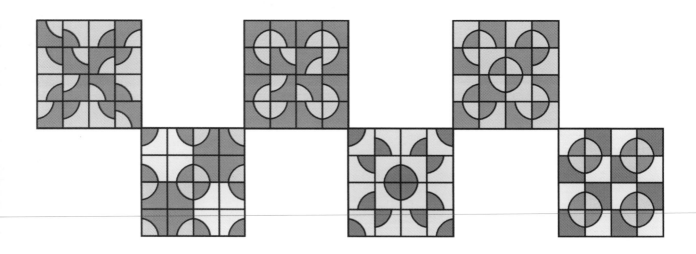

Where each curved square has a finished size of 2":

- 16 curved squares will make an 8" block.

- 4 curved squares will make a 4" block.

Where each curved square has a finished size of 4":

- 4 curved squares will make an 8" block.

This larger size is ideal to try first and *great* for a large quilt!

QH cutting tips for multiple circles

Cut a strip of fabric/freezer paper ¼" larger than the width of your circle. Draw a circle at one end and concertina the strip into a square. Pin to hold together and cut several circles in one go. Mark the centre by pushing a pin through all the layers.

If you have problems marking a circle on fabric, then trace the circle on freezer paper and iron to fabric for use as a temporary cutting guide. Try stacking several layers of fabric to cut in one go.

Cutting instructions

2" unit

Background – cut 5" square.

Circle – cut 2" radius fabric circle.

Freezer paper – cut $1^5/_8$" radius circle.

4" unit

Background – cut 9" square.

Circle – cut 3½" radius fabric circle.

Freezer paper – cut 3" radius circle.

How many units do I need?

1 Choose the block you wish to make.

2 Count the units in the block separately, as dark or light. I count a unit as dark when the background square is dark. They are not always even numbers.

3 Multiply each dark and light unit by the number of blocks you need for your row (see below).

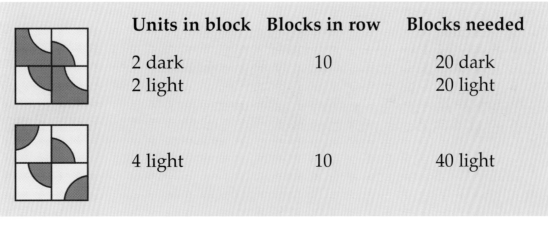

	Units in block	Blocks in row	Blocks needed
	2 dark 2 light	10	20 dark 20 light
	4 light	10	40 light

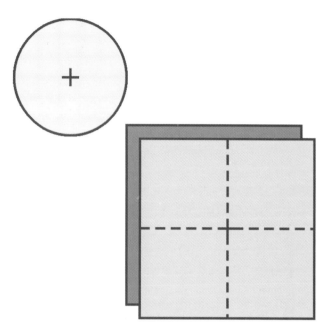

1 Iron two circles of freezer paper together (both with glossy sides underneath) to give a double thickness. Mark centre clearly.

2 Cut squares in required number of light and dark fabrics. Press into a quarter to crease and mark centre.

3 Cut circles in required number of light and dark fabrics (consider using freezer paper as a pattern template so you can avoid marking the fabric).

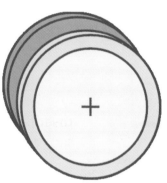

4 Centre a double paper circle, glossy side down onto the wrong side of a fabric circle. Iron to stick the paper to the fabric. Pin through on centre paper mark, to identify and mark the centre of the top fabric.

5 Prepare each of the circles by sewing a gathering thread ¼" in from the edge.

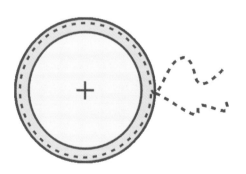

To gather by machine, use the longest straight stitch. Pull up the gathers evenly. You may find it easier to gather in two semi-circles.

To gather by hand use a strong thread and long straight stitch.

Press from the fabric side, taking care that the circle edge is perfectly curved.

6 Centre the circle onto the background by using a pin through the centre back to centre circle. Check that the distance from the circle to the edge is the same on all sides.

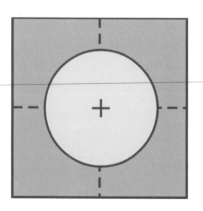

Detail from Rows by any other Name *by Jan Chandler (see p. 110)*

(see p. 110)

QH Tip

If your machine is not happy stitching close to an edge, then stabilize by placing a thin paper under the fabric square as you are sewing.

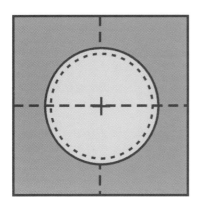

7 Appliqué the circle to the background fabric. Use either a thread matching the fabric circle or a monofilament thread with a neutral thread in the bobbin. Start stitching at a crease line halfway down the square side. Sew either with a small straight stitch as close to the edge as possible. Or select Blind Hemstitch on the sewing machine, setting the stitch width to 1.0 and length to 0.5. Press on the wrong side.

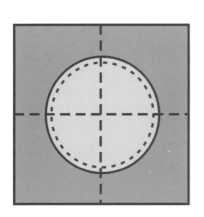

8 Use the rotary cutter to divide the square into quarters along the crease marks. If these have disappeared, simply cut the square into quarters.

9 Cut away and remove the fabric underneath each circle leaving ¼" seam allowance. Gently, remove the freezer paper.

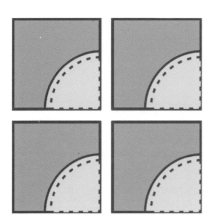

10 Check finished unit measurement (2½" or 4½" square). If necessary, trim to correct size.

11 Follow your chosen block layout diagram to sew the units together.

What if...

 You used a decorative machine stitch to stitch the circle to the square?

Foundation Fun

Sewing on a foundation is a technique that has been used for centuries. But instead of using a fabric as a foundation, I prefer a water-soluble paper. Once you've finished the sewing, dip the block in water – and the paper disappears! 'Easy Tear' vilene or thin paper, which can be torn away after stitching, is a popular alternative.

Complex designs are more accurate when foundation sewn. As long as you can sew on a printed line, accuracy is easy.

The six designs below are from *Electric Quilt 4*, a computer programme which many quilters use for designing quilts. If you have this programme you can print the designs directly onto the paper otherwise you will need to trace or photocopy them.

Have fun taking one foundation block for a row. If you have never tried foundation sewing, practice the tulip design first – this one is the easiest!

The illustration on the previous page shows these six foundation patterns in order of difficulty – with the simplest, the tulip design, first. Below is the template for the tulip design; it's worth noting that the centre of the flower looks good if you make it and the side petals from different fabrics.

On the next two pages you will find full instructions for making a block from this template.

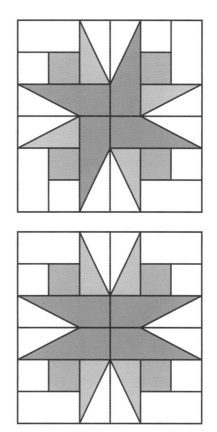

Notice the effect of rotating the block (top right) and mirroring it (right)

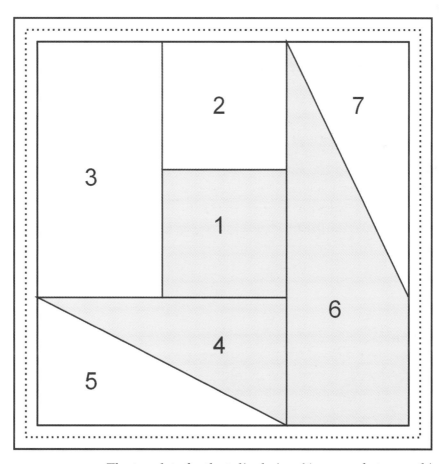

The template for the tulip design. You may photocopy this design for your personal use. The outer, solid square indicates the ¼" seam allowance; the inner, dotted line gives the seam allowance for an 8" block (after the template has been enlarged to 200%).

Foundation Fun (continued)

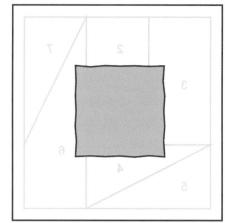

1. The printed foundation designs are for 4″ blocks. Choose a design and make a precise copy either by tracing on to soluble paper, a foundation paper or an easy tear vilene. Alternatively, you can copy on an accurate photocopier or print direct from the Electric Quilt CD. For 8″ blocks you will need to take the pattern to a photocopier where enlargements can be made. Ask for the design to be enlarged to 200%.

2. Cut each fabric patch about 1″ larger than the printed patch. If you are sewing multiples of one design then it is quicker to cut a strip of fabric 1″ wider than the patch measurement. Rough cut pieces from the strip as needed.

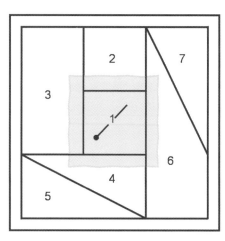

3. When foundation piecing, the sewing is always done from the printed side of the paper but the fabric is placed on the unprinted side.

   Place the first piece of fabric right side up over patch 1 on the unprinted side. It helps to hold foundation up to a light so that you can see through the paper, checking that patch 1 is completely covered by fabric. Pin in place from the printed side.

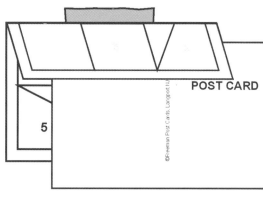

4. Place a postcard along the line that separates patch 1 and 2. Fold the paper back on the line, and hook the add-a-quarter ruler onto the fold so that the ¼″ lip is pushed against it. Trim the exposed fabric by rotary cutting along the add-a-quarter ruler. Alternatively you can use a rotary ruler to trim ¼″ from the fold.

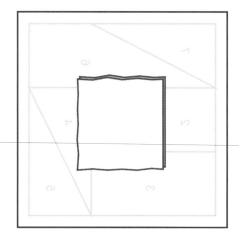

5. Turn fabric side up and with right sides together correctly position fabric patch 2 so one edge matches the trimmed edge. Pin, from the printed side.

QH Tip

Multiple foundations can be made by needle punching the pattern. Layer the traced design on top of several sheets of paper. Use an unthreaded sewing machine to 'sew' along the traced lines.

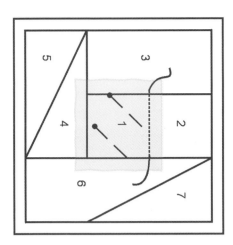

6 You are now going to machine sew on the printed side, stitching on the line that separates patch 1 and 2. An open toed machine foot is useful, as you will be able to see the printed line as you sew. Change to a large needle, use a 90/14 sewing machine needle which makes larger holes. This helps if you have to tear away the paper foundation later. Use a short straight machine stitch (15–20 stitches per inch); this will perforate the paper so it can easily be removed after the block is completed.

Start stitching two or three stitches before the start of the line, and extend your stitching by a few stitches past the line.

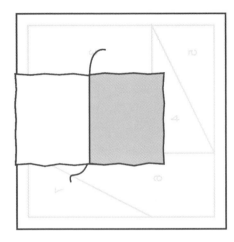

7 On the fabric side press fabric 2 over patch 2. A wooden iron is ideal for pressing the seams flat.

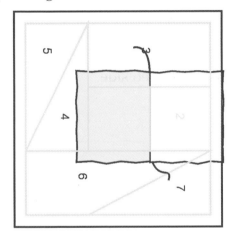

8 Fold back paper on line between patches 2 and 3. Use the add-a-quarter ruler to trim fabric 2.

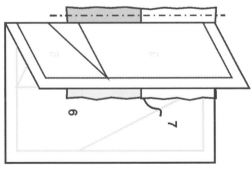

9 Continue adding patches until the block is complete.

Trim the block ¼" from the outside line as you need a seam allowance.

10 Join the blocks to make your row. Gently remove the foundations.

51

Tree

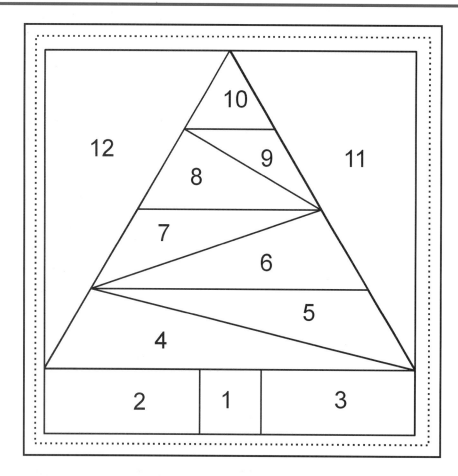

Choose a colour for the trees – this does not need to be green! Then choose several fabrics in this colour to give the tree texture and interest.

What if...

You choose two foundation designs and alternate them in the row?

You alternate with plain blocks of fabric and later use the foundation pattern as a quilting design on the plain block?

Dancing Squares

The centre square is ideal for a 'conversation' print. How about an 'I Spy' row for a child? Cut out various motifs which can be placed in the centre square and then framed with contrasting fabrics.

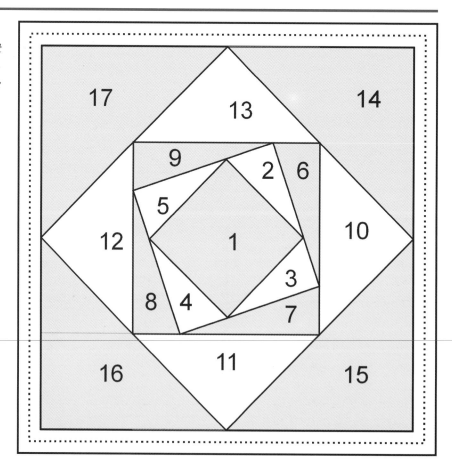

Basket

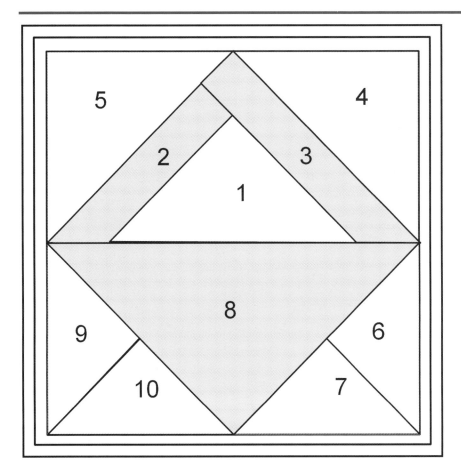

This block has two halves. Each half is stitched before sewing together into the full block. Try appliquéing some flowers in the basket.

(Below) Pieces 9 and 10 must be pieced together before you add them to the block.

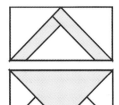

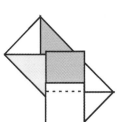

Monkey Wrench (or Snail's Trail)

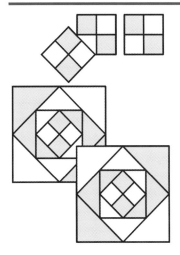

Start with a four-patch block, made from 1½" squares (or use the Chequer board strip method to make several blocks).

Place the completed four patch on the foundation, then sew the remaining patches with the paper. The patches have not been numbered; the sequence works out from the centre four patch in both directions.

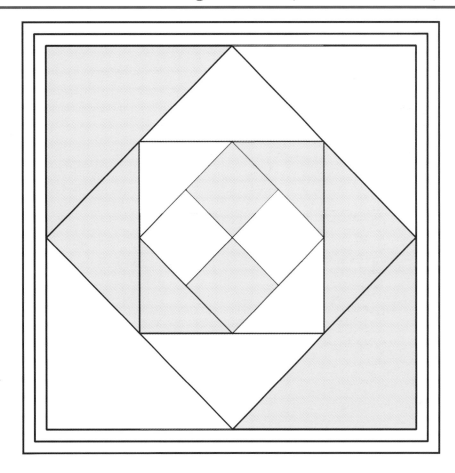

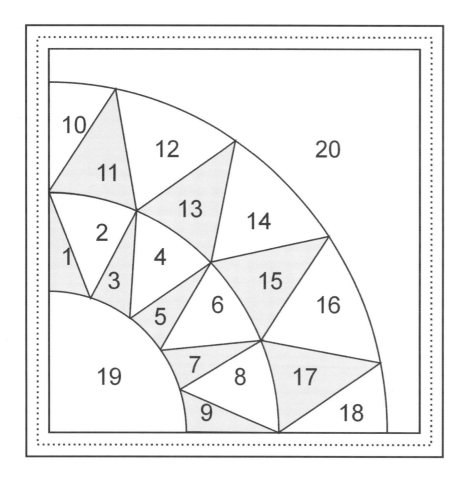

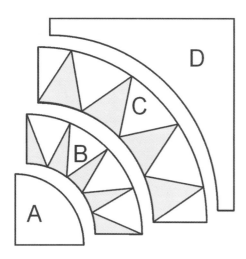

I would recommend this is sewn as an 8″ block, unless you enjoy a challenge!

Foundation piece the two bands separately. Join each curved seam to make the block design. Remember to add the corners. I find marking centre matching points on each seam helps when joining curved seams together.

Two fans joined together can resemble a sun appearing over the horizon.

Cut the foundation paper into four sections. B and C are foundation pieced, and the other two are corner sections to be sewn on after piecing.

If you want to trace this design for an 8″ block, you can use these outlines.

An alternative to adding pieces A and D is to appliqué bands B and C to an 8½″ background (see next section).

Easy Appliqué

When I first started patchwork I avoided sewing appliqué. I thought it was too slow and you needed to be 'artistic'. However, now I love appliqué because I have found techniques that I like using – they are easy. There are so many wonderful patterns and books which give you designs for appliqué that there is no need to draw your own.

I create appliqué simply by cutting out shapes and sewing them onto the background where I feel they look good. Try designing with paper shapes until you feel confident to cut the same shapes in fabric.

For your sew a row, I have given you simple shapes which are easy to appliqué.

These are leaves, a flower, a bow, hearts and stars. You can arrange them separately or have them linked with a trailing 'stem'. I also appliqué on top of patchwork blocks to make them look more interesting!

Sew by hand or machine or use both methods in your row.

If you want a really quick appliqué, use the no sew method.

Detail from Sew-a-Row Funtime
by Anne Smith (see p. 110)

Background fabric

The fabric on which the applique shapes will be sewn can be cut in two ways.

1 Each block in the row can be cut as a separate fabric, or try four similar fabrics sewn together. Cut 1" larger all round – 5" square or 9" square to allow for seam allowances and distortion. Work within the finished size of the block – 4" or 8".

Or 2 Cut the background for the row as one piece of fabric. Calculate the width and length of the row adding 1" all round for seam allowance and distortion. Again, work within the finished size of the row.

Once the background is prepared, choose the appliqué shapes you wish to sew.

Not sure? Cut out shapes in plain or coloured paper and play with them on

your prepared background until you like what you see.

Choose your appliqué technique before cutting out the shapes.

No Sew Appliqué

Ideal for wall hangings and other quilts which will require little handling and washing.

Use a heavyweight fusible web, as the fused fabric edges should not fray even after gentle hand washing. Follow the manufacturer's directions for fusing fabric appliqué shapes to a background fabric.

My favourite no-sew fusible is Steam-a-Seam 2 which has a pressure sensitive adhesive allowing me to position the shapes on my background fabric while it is hanging vertically on a design wall! When I am happy with my appliqué design, I iron the shapes, bonding them in position. No further sewing is required.

Detail from Confetti Hearts *by Lin Patterson (see p.111). What may look like random hearts have in fact been artfully placed...*

Machine Appliqué

Fusible machine appliqué in seven easy steps!

1 Trace shapes onto a double-sided adhesive web.

2 Cut out roughly, outside the drawn shape.

3 With a warm iron bond to the wrong side of fabric.

4 Cut out exactly on the drawn line, no seam allowances!

5 Peel away backing paper.

6 Bond fabric shape to background.

7 Machine stitch around the shape enclosing the raw edges.

Machine appliqué is stronger than hand appliqué, and for many it is faster. The shapes are fused to the background and then a machine stitch is used to finish the edges and prevent fraying.

57

Machine appliqué essentials

Double sided adhesive web

This should be purchased off the roll, as it is easily damaged when folded. It looks like tracing paper, with a fine adhesive web on one side.

You can draw on the paper side, then follow the manufacturer's instructions for bonding the paper to a fabric and the fabric to the background. I like both Bondaweb and Steam a Seam 2.

505 Temporary Spray Adhesive

This is a new alternative to adhesive web and simpler to use. Cut out the fabric shapes, pin them right side down on a large sheet of scrap paper. Spray the wrong side following the manufacturer's instructions. The shapes are now ready to position to the background fabric, the adhesive will hold them in place while you machine stitch.

Thread and needles

Any machine sewing thread can be used. Experiment with the lovely decorative machine stitching threads, as they add to the attractiveness of the appliqué. Some have a sheen; others are variegated, giving bands of different colours, and there is a large selection of metallic threads.

In the bobbin use a lightweight cotton thread (60wt) in a neutral colour. Madeira and YLI have 'bobbinfill' threads made for this purpose. They're cheaper than normal machine threads but only available in neutral colours.

Change your needle to one with a larger eye such as Metallica or Embroidery machine needles when sewing with decorative threads.

Sewer's Aid (see p.13) can be very useful to prevent threads from snapping when you are doing machine appliqué.

Machine Stitching

Most modern sewing machines come with many stitches that can be used for machine appliqué. Try out different stitches and find which of them you and your machine are happiest with, and give the best results.

The four I use most are zig-zag, satin stitch, invisible stitch and blanket stitch. You will need to test each of these stitches on a folded piece of firm fabric, adjusting stitch length, width and tension according to the manufacturer's handbook. Depending on your machine, you may have other embroidery stitches suitable for machine appliqué. Have a play!

Use the appropriate machine foot. A good machine appliqué foot has an open under-channel and is open toed or clear plastic at the front so that you can see where you are stitching.

Always stop with the needle in the down position when you want to turn a corner in machine appliqué. Some machines can be programmed to do this automatically.

I stabilize my sewing by placing a piece of thin paper or Stitch and Tear under my work. This is sewn with the stitch and torn away afterwards.

Popular machine stitches for fused appliqué

Zig Zag stitch – often considered the easiest to sew.

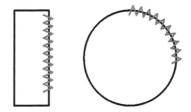

Satin stitch – when the zigzag stitch is set very close together it is called satin stitch and gives a much stronger decorative edge to the shape.

Invisible stitch – can almost look like invisible hand appliqué. Sewn with a good quality monofilament thread, such as YLI. Set your machine for blind hemming.

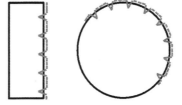

Blanket stitch – used to give a 'folk art' effect.

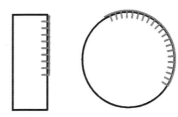

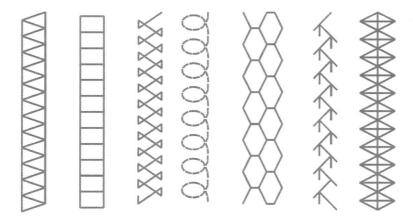

Some favourite machine stitches that can be used for machine appliqué.

59

Hand Appliqué

I like to use an invisible hand appliqué method that does not involve marking the fabric. Instead a soft iron-on vilene (for preference) or my second choice, freezer paper, is used as the pattern template. The template shape is ironed on to the top of the fabric and the seam allowances turned under as you sew. This technique also avoids any mirror image problems – you get the original shape you see!

Preparing for hand appliqué

1 Lay the fusible side of the vilene on the drawing and trace shape with a pencil.

2 Cut out exactly on the drawn line.

3 Using a wool setting, iron the vilene fusible side down to the *right side* of the appliqué fabric.

4 Cut out roughly 1" away from shape edge; this will be trimmed as you sew.

5 Finger crease the seam under and all around the shape; this will help the fabric 'memorise' the crease when later it is needle turned under. The crease line should be at the edge of the vilene; the fabric does not stay under the vilene at this stage.

6 Pin in position on the background using ½" or ¾" appliqué pins. Two or three pins are sufficient.

7 Pin and sew one shape at a time.

QH Tip

Test the vilene on your fabric to ensure it can be peeled off easily without leaving any residue. My favourite is shirt tailor interfacing.

Hints and tips

Use ¾" **appliqué pins**: longer pins catch the thread, and shorter pins are hard to handle. Your **thread** must closely match the appliqué shape, not the background fabric. I like to use 100% cotton thread Mettler 60 as it is fine enough to lie with the fabric. Thread the needle from the spool as this is easier and correctly follows the nap of the thread avoiding any knots as you sew. Cut no more than 18" and knot the cut end.

My favourite **needles** for hand appliqué are Sharps size 10 or 12, the higher the number the finer the needle. I also use Clover gold eye needles size 10 or 12. If you like a longer needle use a Straw needle which helps to turn under the seam allowance as you stitch. Choose a small, sharp pair of **scissors** that cut right up to the tip. I like Clover cutwork scissors and any of the small Gingher scissors.

Ready to Stitch the Invisible Stitch

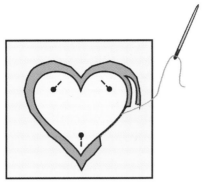

Start sewing at least 1" away from any point, with the seam allowance in that area turned under. Sew in the direction that feels most comfortable. Trim the turned-under seam allowance to ¼" or less, a few inches ahead of the sewing to prevent unnecessary fraying. Start with a knot placed at the back, and pull the needle through the folded edge of the appliqué.

Directly opposite where your needle has emerged, go straight down into the background fabric *only*, come back through the seam allowance fold ¹/₈" away from the first stitch. Use your non-sewing thumb to keep the seam allowance pressed down just ahead of the needle.Use your needle to turn under the seam allowance as you move along.

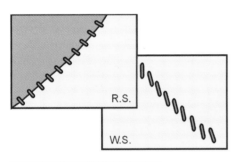

Take only one stitch at a time. A little tug after each stitch helps the thread to sink into the top appliqué fabric, helping the stitch to become invisible. Stitches on the right side should be straight and almost invisible. On the back of your work the stitches look slanted as the stitch travels the ¹/₈".

Stitches need to be closer together on outside and inside points. When you are close to an inside point, clip it to within a few threads of the template and reinforce the fabric with an extra stitch.

To finish, sew a few stitches or use a half hitch knot on the back of your work. Remember practice makes perfect!

A special note about circles

I use a different appliqué method for circles. Iron a freezer paper circle to the wrong side of the appliqué fabric. Cut with a ³/₈" seam allowance. Gather ¼" away from the edge, by hand or use the longest straight machine stitch. Pull up the gathering thread so that it pulls tightly around the freezer paper circle. Then appliqué into place. Remove freezer paper from the back by cutting away the background fabric under the circle, leaving a ¼" seam allowance. (See also pp.46–47.)

QH Tip

If you have problems on the inside V's where you almost run out of fabric as you turn under, then a spot of Fray Check (clear fabric glue) can help.

Easy Stems

Easy stems are cut from the bias of the fabric so they can curve and twist and still lie flat. As they finish up 'stuffed' with four layers of fabric, they sit a little proud from the background and look quite realistic.

Cutting instructions

Use a square of fabric (say 12") with edges cut on the straight of the grain. Make a diagonal (bias) cut from corner to corner.

Place your ruler on the bias cut edge of one triangle and cut 1" wide strips. Bias strips can be used in short lengths, or sewn together for longer lengths.

1 Fold the bias strip in half lengthwise, right sides out. Press gently.

2 Pin into position on the background fabric. You may find it easier to draw a flowing line onto the background fabric before pinning the bias strip.

3 Sew small running stitches or machine stitch ¼" from the fold, along the length of the stem. You can vary the seam allowance to make the stem wide or narrow.

4 Trim the seam allowance to ⅛".

5 Push the folded edge over the raw edge and blind stitch the fold onto the background. The raw edges will be inside the stem and will give it a slightly padded appearance.

QH Tip

A powdered chalk marker, such as the Clover Chaco-liner, is ideal for drawing a temporary flowing vine line on the background fabric. If you are not happy with the line you have drawn, brush off the chalk and start again.

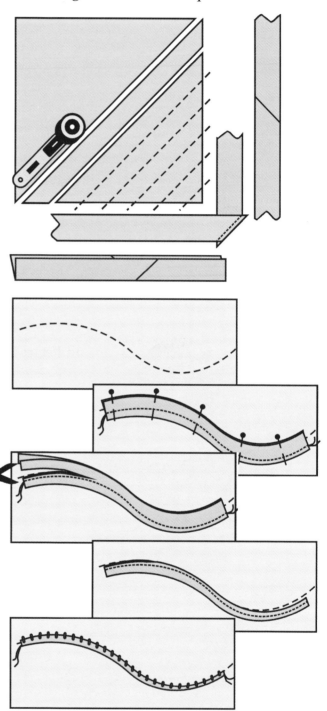

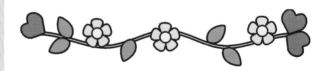

Suffolk Puffs

Suffolk Puffs had to be included in *Sew a Row Quilts* as I and nearly everybody who contributed to this book live in Suffolk. Americans call our Suffolk Puffs 'yo-yos', but we prefer their original name. They are made with gathered circles of fabric and can be used separately or sewn together with spaces between them.

Suffolk Puffs have been used in Sew a Row quilts as flowers, and are fun to embellish with buttons and beads.

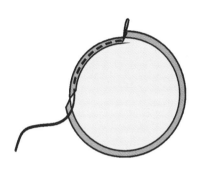

1 Make a freezer paper template or draw circles directly onto the fabric. The cut circles should be twice the size of the finished Suffolk Puff. Try 3" and 4" sizes.

2 A strong thread is needed to gather up the circles. Use a quilting thread or a double length of sewing thread and a short needle.

3 Turn under the circle edge ¼". Knot the thread and start sewing with the knot under the turned edge hem. Sew small straight stitches all the way around the circle turning under the edge as you sew. Overlap the first stitch.

4 Draw up the thread tightly and knot.

5 Flatten the circle so that the 'hole' is in the centre on one side.

6 Appliqué to background fabric, hole side up.

What if...

You sewed on a button or bead to cover the 'hole'?

You used a much smaller circle to place inside the 'hole'? Use the same or a contrasting fabric.

QH Tip

To make buttercups from Suffolk Puffs sew four stitches through the centre, over the edge and into the centre again at the quarters. After each stitch, pull the thread tightly. Finish with several back stitches and a knot.

Appliqué templates

$1\frac{1}{4}$"

In the English Tradition

Traditional English patchwork has always been worked over papers. It is a very accurate but slower method of piecing patchwork. The paper shapes are cut out, the fabric is then tacked over the paper and these patches are oversewn together by hand. This, of course, makes the patchwork very portable – the sort you can sew when you are travelling or just want something to pick up when watching TV in the evening.

I will explain the methods I use for making English patchwork easier and more exciting, but still keeping within the traditional shapes – the hexagon, diamond and Bishop's Mitre. Freezer paper is used instead of paper templates. This has the advantage of adhering to the fabric, eliminating the need to mark and pin fabric. I recommend cutting multiple templates in one go to reduce tedious and sometimes inaccurate cutting.

Hexagons (left), 60° diamonds (below, left) and mitres (below, right) in 1", 1½" and 2" sizes. Sizes are the measurements of one side of the shape. When matching different shapes, choose the same size for an exact fit.

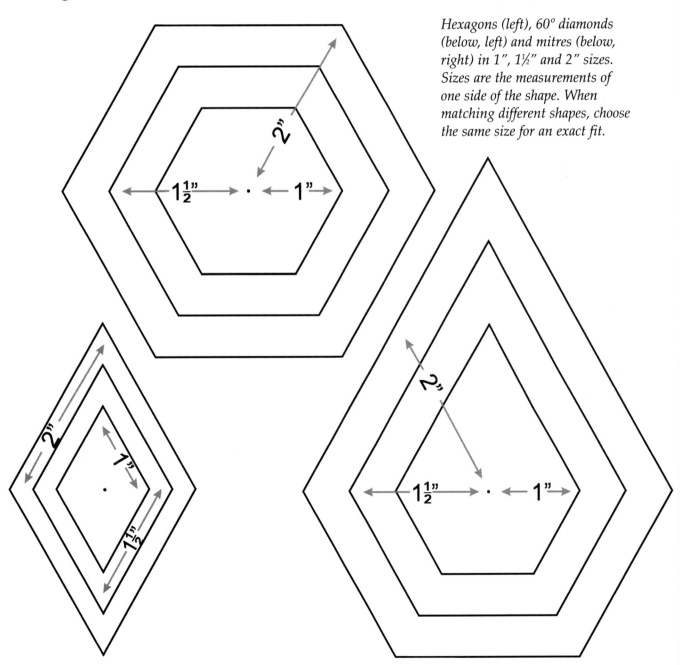

In the English Tradition (continued)

Look at the shapes, and the patterns you can make from these templates, to decide on the design you wish to include in your row.

Some designs are based on a row, and you just keep adding shapes until the row is complete.

Others are block designs where you will have to decide how many shapes are required for the block and then multiply this by the number of blocks in the row. The table below shows you how.

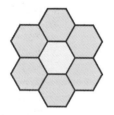

Grandmother's Flower Garden block

7 hexagons x 10 blocks in a row = 70 hexagons needed

Diamond Star block

6 diamonds x 10 blocks in a row = 60 diamonds needed (30 dark, 30 light)

QH Tip

When tracing templates, use Blu-tack to fix the freezer paper to the drawing temporarily.

Use a small ruler when tracing lines as they need to be straight!

Continue the lines just past the template corners so that they cross. The cross marks the exact corner, making cutting out more accurate.

1 Cut a strip of freezer paper the width of the template shape adding ½" for ease. At one end of the strip trace the paper shape on the matt side of the freezer paper. Now concertina the freezer paper behind the drawn shape. Staple the layers together. Cut out the shape, remove the staple and you are ready to go with lots of paper shapes. The good news is that these can each be used several times!

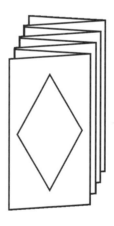

2 Iron the shiny side of the shapes to the wrong side of the fabric leaving enough space between each shape for a 3/8" seam allowance. The wide seam allowance is easier to fold over the paper shapes. For small shapes ¼" is adequate. There is no need to measure this seam allowance, just cut it approximately, letting your eyes judge the distance.

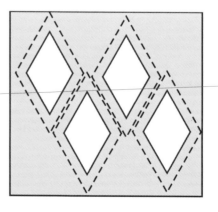

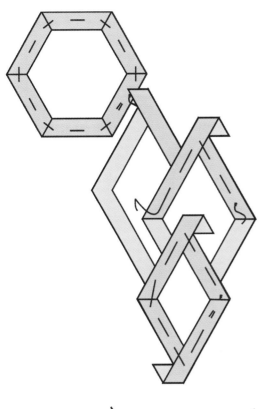

3 Fold the seam allowance over the paper and tack down with a neutral coloured thread. Beware of cheap coloured sewing threads as they can bleed into your fabric.

Start with the knot on the right side as it will be easier to remove later. You will only need to tack one or two stitches on each side of the shape. Make neat corners by taking a stitch over each fold. Always ensure the paper is tightly folded over the paper. End with a couple of fastening off stitches.

Where you have sharp points to tack down, do not tuck in the point, simply leave it free as the tails will nest into each other on the wrong side when sewn together.

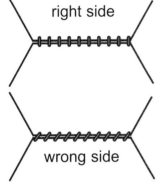

right side

wrong side

Oversew stitch (above): the straight stitches on the right side are barely visible.

4 Once you have tacked enough shapes you can begin to sew them together. Use a good quality cotton thread and knot one end. I prefer to use a short betweens needle to sew the small stitches. Use an overstitch to join the patches together, with a thread that closely matches at least one of your fabrics. Pick up a few threads of fabric from each side with a straight stitch and then travelling less than $1/8''$ over the top of the fabric to pick up the next threads.

5 Pick up two patchwork shapes and hold them right sides together. Start sewing about $1/4''$ from a corner, work two overstitches into the corner, then oversew to the next corner, crossing over the starting stitches. Pick up another patch and continue oversewing. Or you can finish off by oversewing two stitches back from the corner, again crossing over the previous stitches and finishing off.

QH Tip

Spray starch fabrics so they handle better.

For multiple fabric shapes, cut squares of fabric larger than the template plus seam allowance. Layer four to six, ironing a template to the top fabric. Carefully rotary cut, adding seam allowance to template.

Sewing patchwork to a background

I prefer to leave the papers inside my work until after I have sewn it to the background as I have a firm edge to sew.

Prepare the background as described in the section on appliqué (p.56).

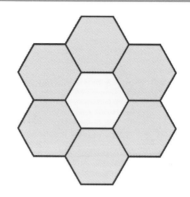

1 Pin and tack the patchwork onto the background making sure you are keeping within the seam allowances.

2 Use an invisible hand appliqué stitch as described on page 61 or one of the machine stitches on page 59.

3 When you have finished the appliqué, remove the tacking stitches and cut the background fabric away from the back, cutting ¼″ inside the stitching line.

4 Remove the papers from the back and reuse them unless the edges are torn.

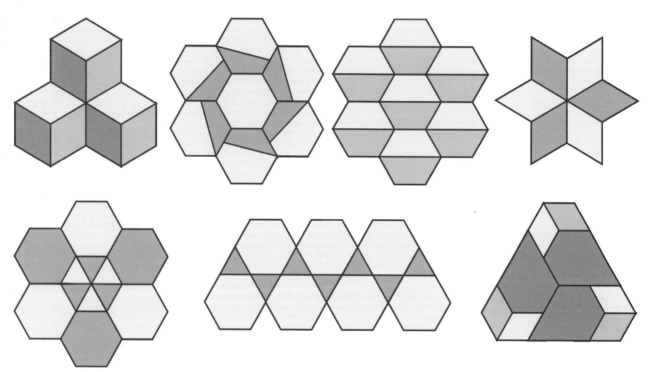

New angles on English Patchwork (above), and in action in Jan Chandler's Rows by any other Name (below, and see p.110).

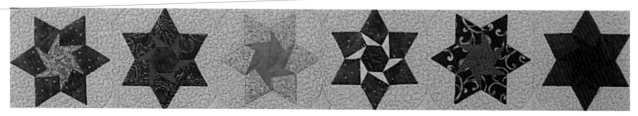

Adding a new angle to English Patchwork

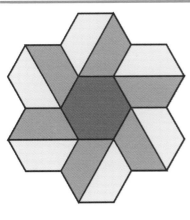

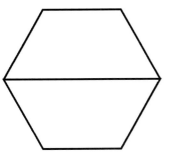

Draw a new line inside the traditional shape and lots of exciting contemporary patchwork begins to appear. You are not increasing the amount of hand sewing by dividing the templates. Simply join two contrasting fabrics with a straight seam before positioning a template and cutting out the shape. Sewing these new angles is easier than it appears.

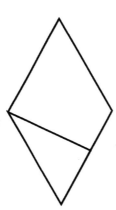

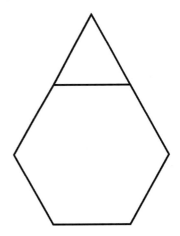

1 Draw a new line on the freezer paper templates. I prefer to draw this from one corner to an opposite corner, or to the middle of a side.

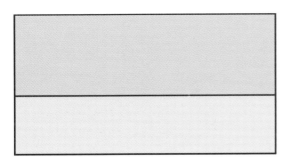

2 To calculate the width of the fabric strips you need to cut, measure from the line to the furthest point on template, add 1". Repeat for second strip measurement. Sew these two strips together with a ¼" seam and press the seam open.

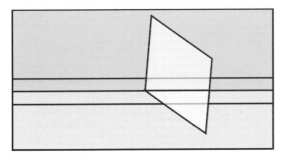

3 Iron the templates onto the fabric strips, with the new lines centred on the open seam.

Continue from instruction **3** for English patchwork.

Dresden Delights

The original Dresden plate designs were based on a circle/plate, folded into segments. I have designed a Dresden daisy, based on a circle, and a Dresden Diamond, based on a diamond, which should be fun to try. Both designs can be used only in the 8" block, but can be sewn as semicircles for a 4" row.

Dresden Daisy – eight spokes

Cutting instructions

Use freezer paper to trace the spoke on the right, as this is your template. Place the paper on the wrong side of your chosen fabric, with the straight of the grain running through the spoke centre, and iron it to the fabric. Use an add-a-quarter ruler lined up against the template, and rotary cut against the ruler. To cut several spokes at once, stack fabric with one paper template on top before cutting. Peel off the paper before sewing; eight spokes make one Dresden Daisy.

1 Fold a fabric spoke right sides together. Press to mark a crease along the fold.

2 Use a short length stitch (15 stitches/ inch) to sew a ¼" seam along the top edge. Start ¼" from fold, reverse stitch to fold and then sew the length of the seam.

3 Clip the folded corner at an angle, and trim seam to ¹/₈".

4 Turn the point using a Purple Thang or stiletto. Make sure you have a good sharp point on the right side.

5 Centre the seam point with the crease running through the middle of the spoke. Press.

70

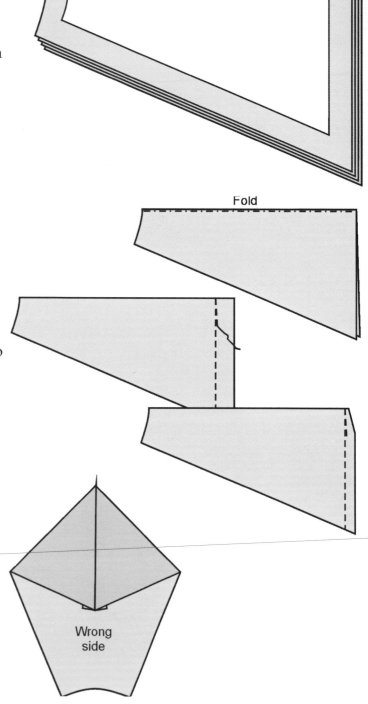

Fold

Wrong side

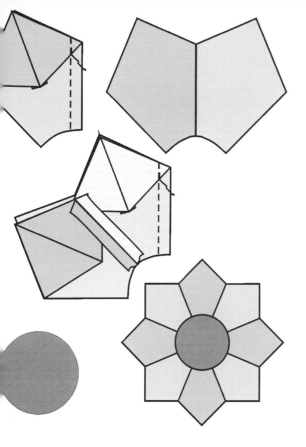

6 Stitch spokes in pairs. Start the stitching ¼″ from the top edges, back stitch to the top edge and then continue down the rest of the seam. Press the seam open.

7 Chain stitch pairs into fours for a semi-circle. These are ideal for a 4″ row.

8 Sew semicircles into circles for an 8″ row.

9 Appliqué on a centre circle (1¼″ radius template), using the template on p.64.

10 Pin and tack to background fabric. Appliqué onto background by hand or machine. By hand, use an appliqué stitch or blanket stitch. By machine, use a medium straight stitch close to the edge, an invisible stitch or decorative edge stitch.

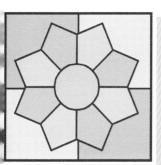

What if...

The background fabric was patched? Four 5″ squares sewn together make an interesting background for a Dresden delight. Once the appliqué is complete, trim the block to 8½″.

Split spoke variation

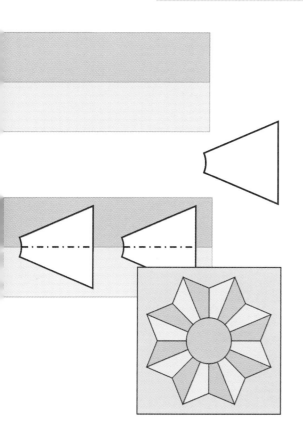

1 Cut two contrasting strips 2¼″ wide. Sew together along their length with a ¼″ seam.

2 Press seam open.

3 Draw a line through the centre of the spoke template, as in the diagram.

4 Iron freezer paper spoke to wrong side of strip set, lining marked line on spoke with the centre of the seam.

5 Cut out fabric spokes and follow steps in Dresden Daisy.

Dresden Diamond

Originally based on a diamond shape this design is a little more challenging!

There are twelve spokes. The four large ones are sewn in the same way as the Daisy spokes. The remaining eight are pairs which are reverse images of one another.

1 Cut four spokes based on template C by tracing the template onto freezer paper, ironing it on to fabric, and cutting out with the add-a-quarter ruler.

2 Follow instructions 1–5 for the Dresden Daisy.

3 If you are using one fabric for the template D pair of spokes, then fold right sides together and press. If you are using two fabrics, lay them right sides together and press.

4 Iron template D onto the layered fabric, and cut out. You should have a pair of spokes that are mirror images of one another.

5 With template D still in place, fold side 'a' towards the other long side along the dotted line.

6 Follow instructions 2–4 for the Dresden Daisy.

7 Align the raw edges on the diagonal side seam so that the point is in line with the crease. Check the spoke alignment by placing on template E.

8 Stitch template D spokes in pairs, straight edges together. Start the stitching ¼" from the top edges, back stitch to the top edge and then continue down the rest of the seam.

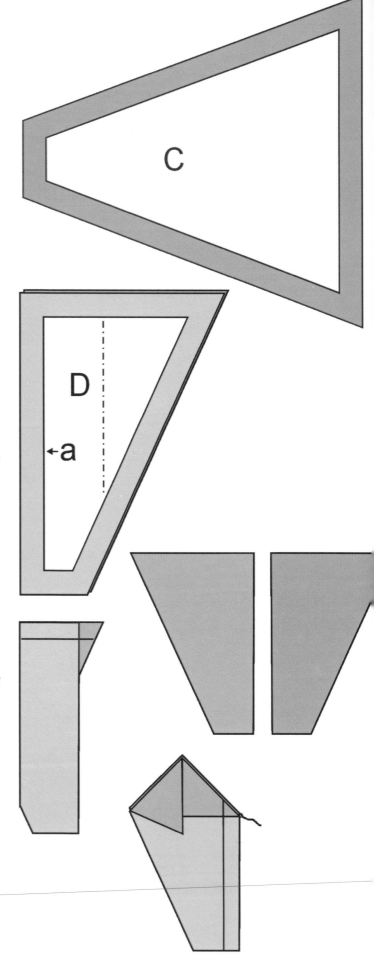

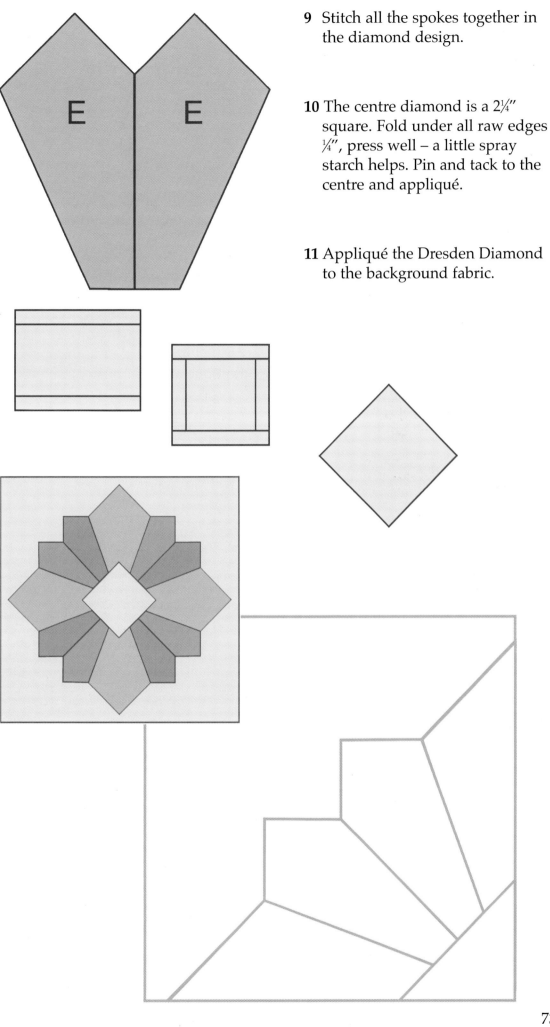

9 Stitch all the spokes together in the diamond design.

10 The centre diamond is a 2¼″ square. Fold under all raw edges ¼″, press well – a little spray starch helps. Pin and tack to the centre and appliqué.

11 Appliqué the Dresden Diamond to the background fabric.

Creative Stencils

Making your own stencils

'A quilting stencil gives you more than quilting designs!'

The inspiration for this chapter comes from the traditional 'strippy' quilts that have been made for centuries in the northeast of England, where I spent my childhood.

For generations northern quilters sewed simple rows of vertical strips in two contrasting fabrics and then embellished them with elaborate hand quilting.

Quilting designs can be seen in many books and can be purchased as plastic stencils from any well-stocked quilt shop.

For many years I have encouraged students to use the simpler designs for many sewing techniques – 'A quilting stencil gives you more than quilting designs!'

On the following pages you will find illustrations of designs that look equally good as vertical or horizontal rows of quilting, followed by instructions for using them to create Italian corded quilting, reverse appliqué and bias strip appliqué.

The designs work well as a sashing to separate and unify your patchwork rows. With this in mind I have designed stencils with a 4" or 2" repeat. An 8" width would normally be considered too clumsy in size.

North Country 'strippy quilts' were pioneering Sew a Rows!

QH Tips

Always test fabric markers on a spare piece of fabric to check that they can be erased.

Chemical pens are not recommended; they could eventually damage the fabric.

Preparing the Design

I like to draw the design onto a piece of freezer paper which has been cut to the exact measurement of the row.

I start to draw from both ends, so that the design meets in the centre. I have found that if I start at one end, then somehow the design does not quite fit when I reach the other end!

By drawing from both ends, I can use a little creativity to help them meet in the centre. Once I am happy with the design I use a black pen to outline the original pencil lines so that I can see the design clearly.

I then iron the freezer paper to the wrong side of the top fabric and trace the design lines onto the fabric. If I have problems seeing the lines, I either tape the fabric to a sunny window or use a light box.

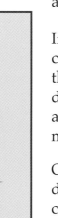

If I am using a ready made plastic stencil then I can lay this directly onto the fabric and draw through the empty spaces which make the design. Again, I always start at each end, using a little creativity in the centre where the design meets.

Once the stencil is removed, the lines you have drawn through the stencil will need to be connected so that they flow in a continuous line.

You can make quilting designs

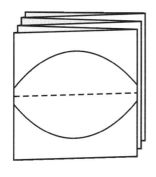

Remember making paper dolly chains at school? Cut a length of paper the height and length of your row. Concertina the length of paper into a square. Draw a design on the top, taking the folds into consideration. Cut and unfold to reveal the repeated design. Use this as an outline for your design.

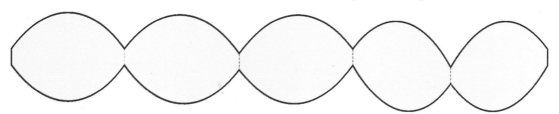

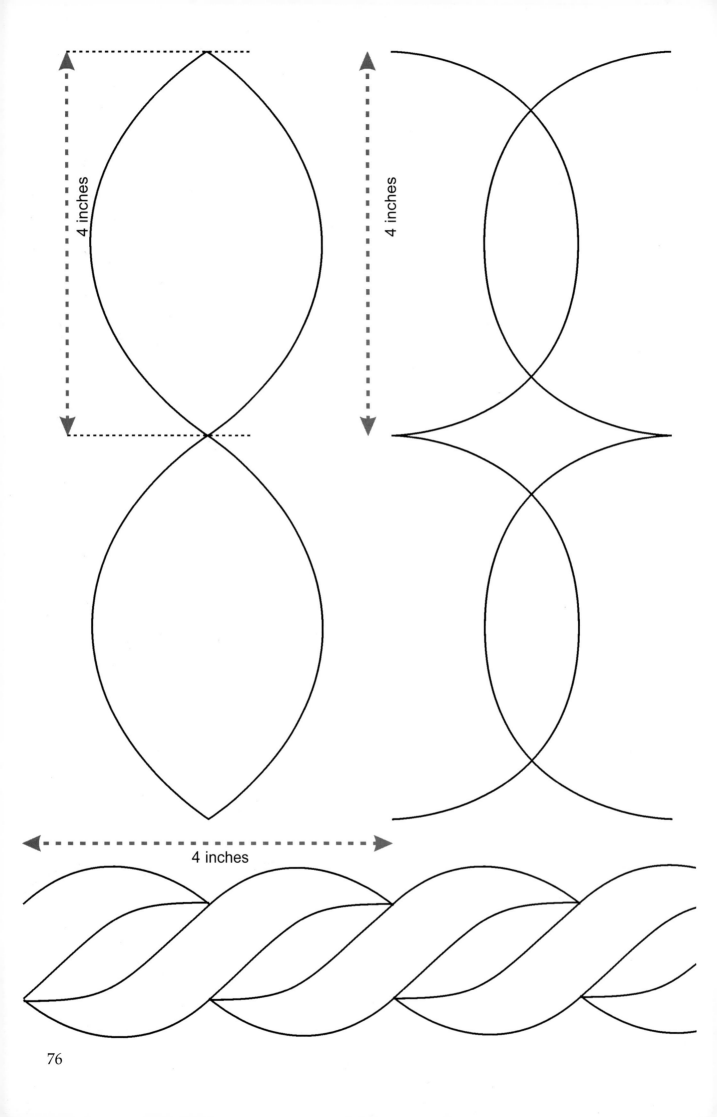

4 inches

4 inches

4 inches

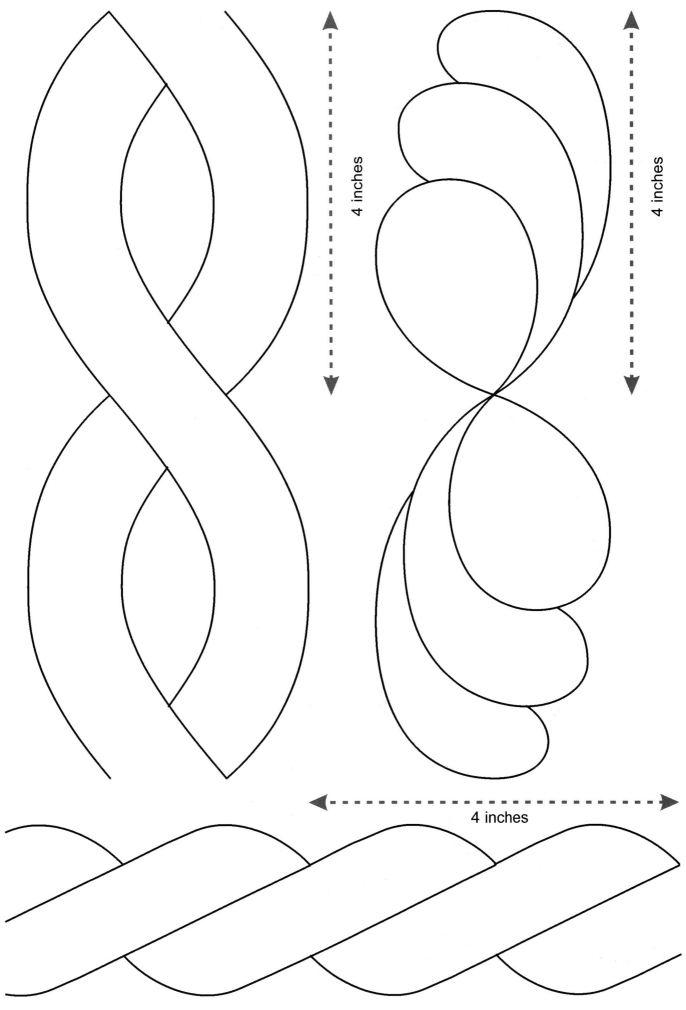

4 inches

4 inches

4 inches

Using creative stencils

Using the stencil on the previous page, Claire Frew has made amazingly vibrant clouds using bias tape appliqué to outline stained glass infills! (You can see this design on her quilt, illustrated on the front cover.)

Drawing a second series of arcs ¼" outside the stencil from page 76 converts it to a suitable pattern for Italian quilting. This design is used in Jan Allan's Shush (see p.80).

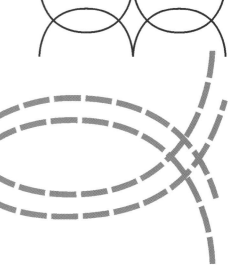

By now you will have noticed that mix and match is the name of the game. Pat Boyes' bias strip appliqué uses a simple curved template together with a 2" diamond shape.

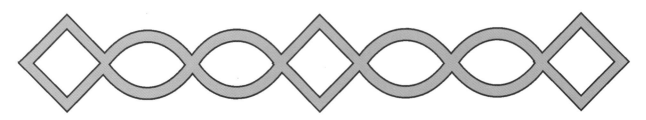

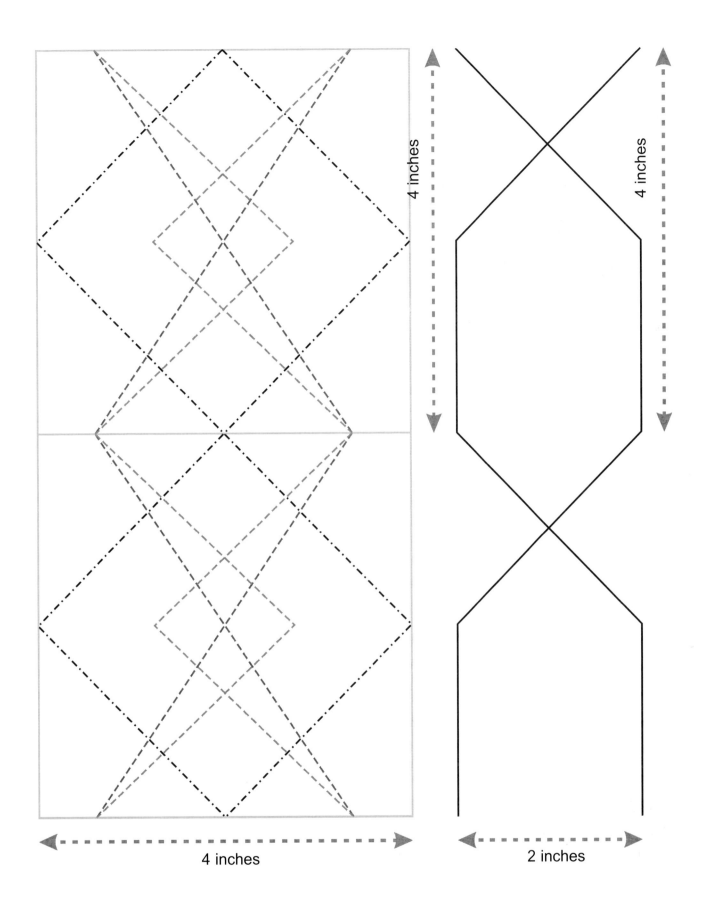

4 inches

4 inches

4 inches

2 inches

79

Italian Corded Quilting

Two layers of fabric are joined by stitching two parallel lines with a running or back stitch. Machine stitches can also be used. Cord or yarn is then inserted into the channel. This gives a raised design which I have found is one of the most admired forms of quilting.

Two layers of fabric are needed. The top layer will show the quilting to best effect if it is a plain/solid, not heavily patterned fabric. The second layer is underneath and should be a light cotton: USA Muslin is ideal.

Calculate the width and length of the row including an extra 1" all round. Cut the two fabrics the same size.

I use a commercial quilting wool as the yarn and either a tapestry needle or trapunto needle to insert the yarn. If you wish you can use a thin cord. Make sure that the yarn or cord is pre-shrunk.

1 Draw the quilting design onto the top fabric.

2 Tack the two layers together, avoiding stitching near the marked design.

3 Stitch on the drawn line. A second line will need to be stitched ¼" from the first, so that a channel is formed. Stitching can be by hand or machine. I prefer to use a quilting thread when hand stitching, as the small running stitches or back stitches need to be strong.

4 Insert the yarn.

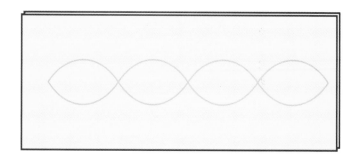

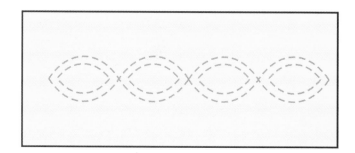

Inserting the yarn

Cut lengths of yarn, no more than 18" in length.

With the underside facing you, insert the threaded needle at the end of the channel inside the stitching lines, leaving a ¼" tail at the beginning. Do not go through to the front fabric.

Pull the yarn gently. Run the needle as far as possible, bringing it through to the wrong side and reinsert it into the same

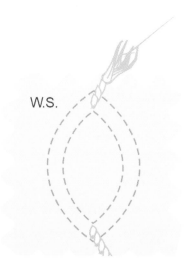

W.S.

W.S.

hole, leave a small loop at each exit point. The loops will allow for stretch and shrinkage. If you have a curve or point it is easier to take shorter lengths and keep re-inserting the needle.

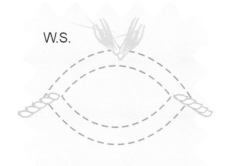

W.S.

Before the length of yarn runs out, bring the needle through to the wrong side and cut the yarn close to the fabric.

Continue with a new length of yarn starting at the same hole you finished previously.

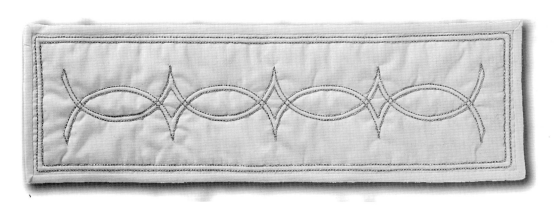

Italian corded quilting techniques are beautifully demonstrated in this border hanging, Shush *by Jan Allen (6"x 18").*

Blocking the Corded quilting

The tugging needed when you insert the yarn can pull the fabric out of shape. Pull on your work in both bias and straight directions to allow the yarn to settle into the channels. If there is distortion, blocking is important.

1 Pin your work onto a board. I lay a towel on a carpet and pin with strong quilters' pins every 2".

2 With your iron set on steam, hold the iron just above your work, allowing the steam to be absorbed by the fabric. The iron should not touch the fabric.

3 Let the block dry completely before removing the pins.

Trim the work to the measurement needed for your row.

Bias Tape Appliqué

Bias tape is used to emphasise the quilting design instead of quilting stitches. If you wish you can place contrasting fabrics in the centre design areas to give a stained glass effect. I like to use a fusible tape made by Clover as it saves time and scorched fingertips! This tape is made from a closely woven cotton and is available in a number of colours. It has a fusible underside which when ironed in position adheres to the base fabric, eliminating the need for tacking. Alternatively you can make your own bias tape using bias bars or bias makers.

Inserting centre shapes – optional

1 Trace the inside design shape onto freezer paper.

2 Cut out paper shape.

3 Iron onto chosen fabric and cut out using the edge of the freezer paper as a template. Several shapes can be cut out at the same time by pinning several fabrics together before cutting. Remember the freezer paper can be peeled off the original fabric and used again several times.

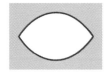

4 Place the fabric insert into position on the right side of the background fabric. It will need to be held in place temporarily. I use a spray fabric adhesive or Roxanne's Baste-It glue.

If you prefer, tack into position. The raw edges of the shape will be covered by the bias tape.

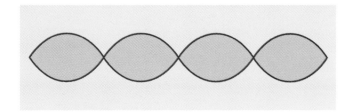

Sewing the bias tape

Lay the tape directly on the drawn line. I always start at a crossing point so that the second tape that crosses over will hide the join. If you run out of tape before you reach the end then finish and re-start on a crossover point. On curves, the bias allows the tape to lie flat. At points, fold the tape into a mitre before changing direction. Sew in place by hand or machine. By hand use an invisible appliqué stitch; by machine, use a small, straight stitch close to the edge of the tape. Repeat the stitching close to the edge on the opposite side of the tape.

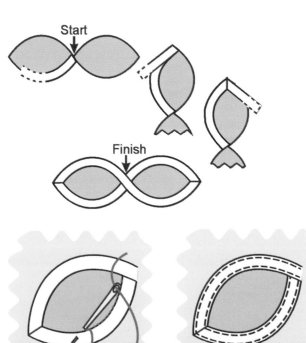

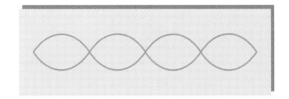

Reverse appliqué

The top fabric is cut away to reveal a second fabric underneath. The centre shapes inside the stencil designs are ideal for cutting away to reveal other fabrics.

1 Cut two pieces of fabric the measurements required for the row, remembering to add an extra inch all round.

2 Draw the design on the right side of the top fabric.

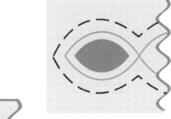

3 Place the second fabric right sides up underneath the top fabric. Tack together just outside design.

4 Only shapes which are enclosed by the design can be cut to reveal the second fabric.

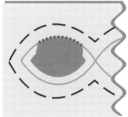

Sewing by hand

Using a sharp pair of small scissors and cutting the top fabric *only*, cut away one centre shape, to within ¼" of the drawn line. Turn top fabric under and slip stitch the fabric on the drawn line. Use a thread that matches the top fabric, making your stitches as invisible as possible. Keep your stitches close together at points. Only cut and stitch one shape at a time to keep your work stable and minimise fraying.

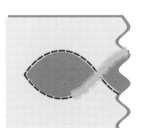

Sewing by machine

Use a straight stitch to sew on the drawn line. Cut away the inside shapes, top fabric only, close to the stitched line. Use a zigzag or satin stitch to cover the raw edges. Trim the row to the correct size before using in your quilt. Admire the lovely fabric shapes that have been revealed from your original quilting stencil!

What if...

The underneath fabric shaded into several colours along its length?

Many different fabrics were joined in a length before placing underneath?

The raw edges were left to fray? You would still need the straight stitch for stability.

83

Finishing the Quilt

This is the moment you have been waiting for – sewing those rows together and finishing the quilt!

Arranging the rows

Spend some time looking at your patchwork and arranging the rows. Laying the rows out on a bed or floor is fine, but it is even better to use a design wall. I use 100% cotton wadding as my design wall, and this can eventually end up inside the quilt as my wadding. Pin a design wall up in a room where you can stand back to admire your work. I peg my design wall to the curtain rail – make sure you have good lighting! Now ask yourself the following:

● Do I want the rows to be horizontal or vertical?

● Do I want to separate the rows with a sashing – and if so, will it use strips of fabric or a simple patchwork?

● Does the patchwork need to fill a row, or can a piece of fabric be used to complete the row?

● Does the quilt look 'balanced' in colour and design? Squint, or use a reducing glass, to help you see the balance.

● Do I need borders around the quilt?

● Is it the size I want?

Borders

A quilt can be brought up to the size you want by adding borders. Border strips cut from one fabric only can be sewn to all four sides of your quilt or try something more challenging.

Patchwork borders can be made using any of the techniques in this book. I use the 4" block size. Measure the sides of the quilt and if they are not divisible by 4 add a plain border first of 1–3". My rule is to oversize this border and cut it down once I have fitted the patchwork border to the quilt. I don't do complicated maths and there is no need for you to either!

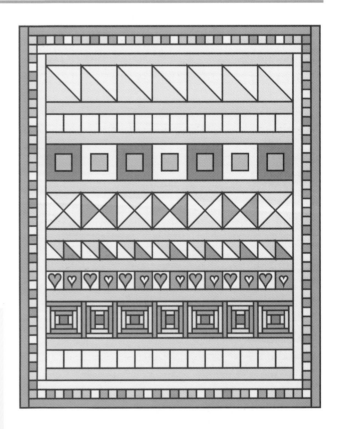

QH Tip

Using a sashing to separate the rows means less matching of points and seams is needed.

Fit borders to the sides of the quilt first, then top and bottom, as it is easier on the eye to follow the straight seam across the quilt.

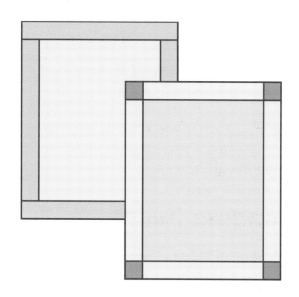

Use cornerstones both as a border feature and to make it easier when designing a patchwork border.

Quick strip pieced border

A great way of using up those left over pieces of fabric from the quilt top. This makes a quick and unifying effective border as it reflects the fabrics used in the centre patchwork.

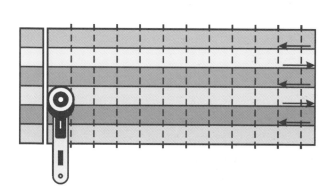

1 Cut 2½″ straight strips from various fabrics.

2 Sew together along their length into a strip set, alternating the sewing direction.

3 Press seams in one direction.

4 Cut 2½″ border strips at right angles to strip set.

5 Join end to end for length required for borders.

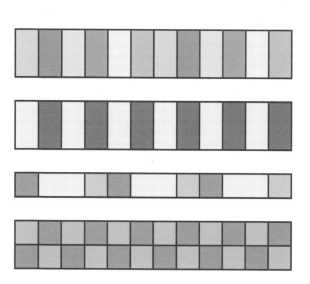

What if...

You cut 4½″ border strips from the strip set? The border would have rectangles, not squares.

You only used two or three fabrics and arranged them in sequence? Vary the width of the initial strips.

You used four patch?

Preparing the backing

The quilt backing needs to be at least 3″ larger than the quilt top on all sides. I usually recommend 100% cotton backing. If I have used silk for the patchwork then I prefer silk as a backing. It is also fun to back a quilt with a polyester fleece, as this gives a cuddly, warm feel without the need for wadding. The quilt *Harvest Home* has been backed with fleece.

Cotton fabric is available in 90″ and 108″ widths. You can patch together a backing with fabric that is left over from your quilt top, or use two quilt tops for a reversible quilt. Reversible quilts work well as lap quilts.

If you have two lengths of fabric that require joining for the quilt back, you do not really want a central seam. It is stronger and more attractive to have a central panel with two side panels.

A quick way to sew this is to place the two lengths right sides together and stitch a seam well inside the selvedge on both long sides. If the selvedge is tight, and distorting the seam, it should be clipped or removed. Cut up the centre of *one* length only. Open and press out the seams.

Layering and joining the quilt layers

The traditional way

Traditionally the rows are joined and borders added to complete the quilt top before placing it onto the backing and wadding. Quilting or tying is needed to hold the layers together.

1 Place the backing wrong side up on a large, clean table. Use masking tape to anchor the backing to the table, stretching the backing but taking care not to pull it out of shape. The backing

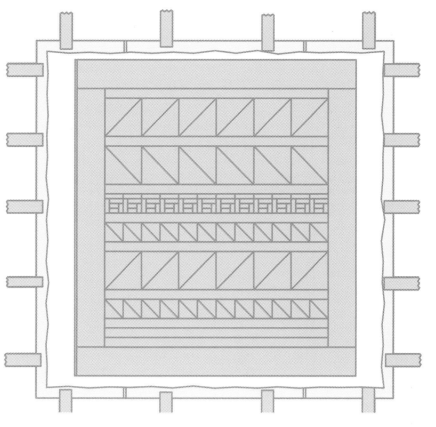

can also be pinned to a carpeted floor using strong quilt pins, stabbed at an angle into the carpet.

2 Place the wadding on top, smoothing it over the backing.

3 Place the pressed and tidied quilt top (no stray threads), right side up on the wadding. Centre the top, making sure the rows are parallel to the edges of the backing.

4 The layers need to be tacked temporarily for tying or quilting.

Tacking/basting methods

Use one of these methods to keep the quilt layers together:

a **Hand tacking:** Tack by hand using a long straw needle and a light coloured tacking thread. Cut a very long thread and start in the centre, tacking out to the edge with half the length. Pick up the other half of the thread, and tack from the centre out to the opposite edge. Tack a grid of 6" parallel lines over the whole quilt. I don't use this method if I am going to machine quilt, as the tacking stitches tend to get caught up with the machine stitches.

b **Safety pins:** Use rustproof 1" safety pins spaced 3–4" apart. Again, pin in the centre and work towards the outer edges, smoothing the quilt top out as you pin. A good method for machine quilted tops, as you can move and remove the safety pins as you quilt.

c **The Quiltak System:** My favourite method as it is relatively quick and painless. It can be used when preparing for any of the quilting methods. A gun is used to 'shoot' small plastic tacks through the quilt layers. I always use a plastic grid placed between the table and the backing to protect the needle and work surface from damage.

d **Temporary adhesive spray:** Recently several spray adhesives have been developed especially for quilters. They provide a temporary stickiness for the layers without gumming up needles when quilting. The adhesive is very light. Follow the instructions provided by the manufacturer.

Layering with sew and flip

Use this method to assemble and quilt a large quilt in 4–5 hours! The backing and a cotton wadding only are joined. The rows are sewn into place one or two at a time using a sew and flip method. This has the advantage of machine quilting the rows as you assemble them into a quilt. No further quilting is required. It is essential to use a walking foot attachment on your machine to prevent the layers shifting.

1 Place the backing wrong side up, on a clean large table. Use masking tape to anchor the backing to the table, stretching the backing but taking care not to pull it out of shape. The backing can be pinned to a carpeted floor using strong quilt pins. Temporarily tack the wadding to the backing using one of the methods described.

2 On the wadding draw a grid of parallel lines, this gives guidelines when placing the rows. I slide a rotary cutting ruler to draw lines parallel to the sides, both horizontally and vertically. Draw at least four lines in each direction as guides to keep your rows straight.

3 Pin the centre patchwork row right sides up in the centre of the wadding. Pin into position using the nearest guideline to keep the row straight. I pin using flower pins at right angles to the row, pinning every 2–3"; these are left in place whilst stitching and only removed as my machine foot approaches.

4 Pin the adjoining row right sides down on top of the centre row.

5 Using a walking foot stitch a ¼" seam along the length of the patchwork. Gently press the row away from the centre.

6 Continue adding the rows, working from the centre out in both directions. Remember to remove any safety pins and tacks as you go.

7 Borders can also be added using this sew and flip method.

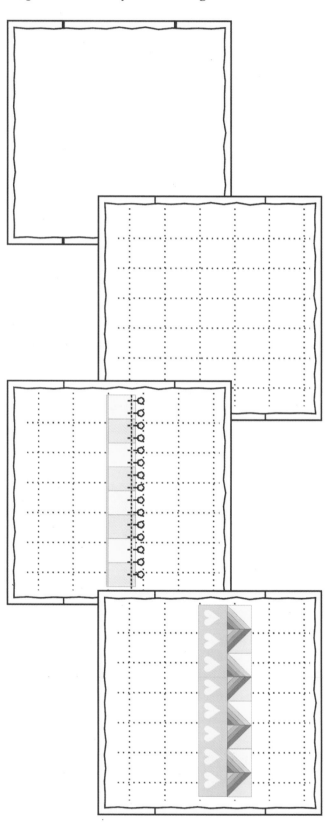

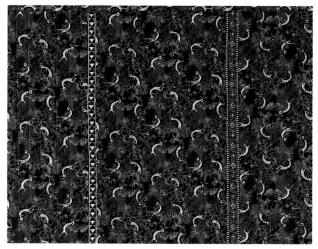

Reverse (above) of Frozen Music *by Marion Barnes (56" x 80") showing Marion's method and (below) the front of the quilt.*

This is the method used for the quilt *Frozen Music*. Marion wanted to machine quilt smaller sections of her quilt and then stitch them together. Quilting sections of a quilt and then joining it together is ideal for quilters who find a large quilt difficult to handle.

1 Mark wadding as instructed under the sew and flip technique.

2 Cut wadding and backing into three equal lengths/sections.

3 Tack a length of wadding and backing together for each section.

4 Sew and flip the rows, working from the centre out on all three sections.

5 Quilt as required.

6 Join the sections together by sewing the adjoining patchwork rows only.

7 Place the joined sections patchwork side down. Let the two edges of wadding overlap and cut through the centre of both layers to trim away excess wadding. The wadding should now lie flat with the edges butted together. These should be herring-bone stitched. Repeat with the backing fabric.

If your walking foot does not have a ¼" guide then use ¼" masking tape as a guide. The tape can be laid on top of the pins, which can still be removed as you sew without disturbing the tape.

8 Cover the seams on the back of the quilt with an applied contrasting strip of fabric. Alternatively, the backing fabric raw edge can be turned under and folded over the adjoining raw edge. Sew along the overlapping seam with an invisible hand stitch or slip stitch.

Quilting

Quilting refers to the stitching used to hold all the quilt layers together, and is used to decorate and enhance the quilt top. If you have used the sew and flip method for sewing together patchwork rows then it is may not be necessary to quilt, as you have already 'machine quilted' along the seams. I prefer to keep my hand quilting for the areas that really show!

If you want the quilting completed quickly, or don't enjoy quilting, consider using the utility stitches (see p.92).

I have recommended some excellent quilting books in the further reading section on p.107 – and remember, any of the quilting stencils and appliqué shapes in this book can be used as quilting designs.

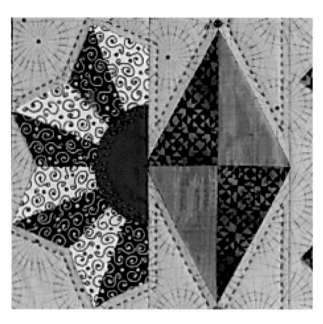

Hand quilting

This is a short running stitch, using a single strand of quilting thread that goes through all the layers of the quilt and can be seen on the back. Use a short needle (betweens size 10), quilting thread and thimbles.

1 Thread the needle with about 18" of thread. Make a small single knot at the end of your thread.

2 Insert the needle through the top fabric only about 1" from where you wish to start stitching, pulling the needle out at the starting point. Gently tug on the thread until the knot pops through your top fabric and lies between the layers, where it is concealed.

Flight of Fancy *by Pat Boyes (41"x 64"), and (above, left), details of the beautiful hand quilting.*

90

3 Sew short *even* stitches using a rocking motion, so the needle goes straight through all the layers. Take two or three stitches at a time, pushing the needle with your thimble.

4 To end a line of quilting, make a small knot on the surface of the quilt. Insert the needle into the wadding running a 1″ stitch through the top and wadding only. Cut the thread on the surface of the quilt, pull the thread slightly as you cut so that it disappears into the layers and is concealed.

(Below) Beautiful machine quilting from Rows by any other Name *by Jan Chandler of Quilting Solutions (see p.110).*

Machine quilting

Any machine threads can be used for machine quilting. Until you feel confident use a thread that blends in with the quilt top as it will disguise any imperfect stitching. As you become more expert, experiment with the gorgeous threads that are now available. I find that a special quilting machine needle does help to keep those stitches even.

Use a walking foot for straight quilting lines. This useful attachment evenly feeds the quilt through the machine preventing shifting of the quilt layers as you stitch. A slightly longer length stitch is used. When turning a corner, lower the needle into the fabric before raising the presser foot and turning the quilt.

A darning foot attachment is ideal for curved or free motion quilting designs. By setting the stitch width and length dials to zero and dropping the feed dog on the machine you can guide your quilting in any direction without ever turning your quilt. To start, bring the lower thread to the top surface to prevent any tangling underneath and hold both threads for a few stitches. Then, keeping the machine at a constant even speed, move the quilt to let the needle stitch a curved design. A popular design is to 'meander' over the quilt stitching round squiggles that should not cross over each other.

It is important to relax when you are machine quilting. Gripping and moving the quilt can make you tense. Some people find it easier to use quilting gloves with rubber grippers on the surface, others like the horseshoe hoops which hold the quilt like a 'steering wheel'. You will bless anything that makes the job easier.

Fasten off the threads by sewing them back through the surface and into the quilt layers.

Utility Quilting

✗ **Utility quilting** is faster than traditional hand quilting. It has been used for many centuries to finish quilts quickly, so they could be used when the cold winters arrived. The finished quilts are sturdy, and have added surface texture.

✗ **Thicker threads are used** for utilitarian quilting, such as sashiko, perle cotton, top stitching and embroidery threads. Large needles are needed for the thicker threads – chenille, milliners and 3″ doll needles. The longer needles are ideal for travelling the distance in the wadding, a requirement of most of the stitches.

Detail of Kathleen Brennan's Barbican Rows (23″x 33″); *a variety of utility stitches in variegated jeans thread brings the patchwork colours into the background.*

Beginning your Stitching

Burying a knot in the wadding by popping it through the quilt top, as is done in hand quilting, does not work well when using thicker threads. The knots are so large they can damage the top fabric. Instead use one of the following methods.

No knot method. Use a thread twice as long as you consider comfortable. Start your stitch by pulling through half the thread only, and stitch until this is used. Later go back and thread up this excess length and continue your stitching.

Backstitch once or twice on the edge of the quilt where the binding will cover it later.

Ending your Stitching

After completing the last stitch, take a tiny back stitch on top of or very close to the last stitch, splitting the thread as you return to the surface. Insert the needle into the wadding very near to where the thread exited and travel for approximately 2″; do not go through to backing. Return to the quilt top, hold the thread taut, and clip it close to the surface of the quilt. The thread end will be trapped in the quilt layers.

Big Stitch

Sew a quilting / running stitch with big stitches ¼″ long. Keep the stitches even in length. Follow a marked quilting pattern or sew free hand without marking the quilt top.

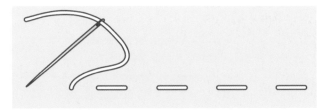

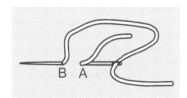

Tying

Start with a very long thread, and insert the needle at A leaving a 2″ thread. Stitch ¼″ through all the layers to B. Insert the needle again at A, emerging again at B.

Travel 3–4″ over the top of the quilt. Repeat until the thread is used.

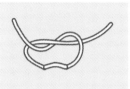  

Cut the top threads apart, tie a reef knot at each stitch, and cut off excess threads to ¼″ or longer.

What if...

You include a button when tying each stitch?

Bar Tacks or Seeding

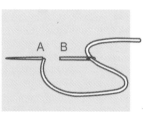

Start at A.
Backstitch ¼″ to B.
Go through all the layers, emerging at A.
From A back stitch a second time to B.

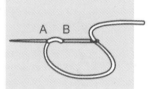

Now go into the wadding *only* and travel to the starting point of the next stitch.

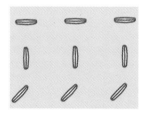 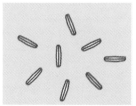

The stitches can be arranged horizontally, vertically, diagonally...

...or at random.

Cross Stitch

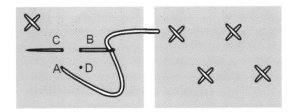

Start at A.

Take a stitch through all the layers at B, coming up at C.

Insert the needle at D and travel through the wadding *only* to the starting point of the next stitch.

Crow Footing

Start at A.

Hold the thread down with your thumb and insert the needle at B.

Go through all the layers bringing the needle out at C.

Pull up the thread to form a V shape.

Insert the needle at D, on the opposite side of the thread from C.

Travel through the wadding only to the starting point of the next stitch.

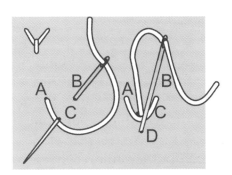

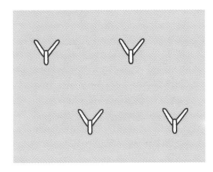

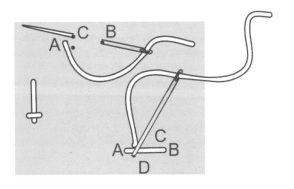

Mennonite Tack

Start at A.

Take a ½" back stitch to B.

Go through all the layers, coming up at C a few threads before the starting point.

Insert the needle at D so that the thread goes over the top of the A–B thread.

Travel through the wadding only to the starting point of the next stitch.

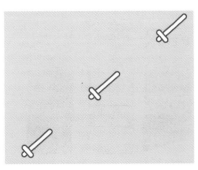

Reversible Binding

I like to use a reversible binding when I have made a reversible quilt. Lap quilts in particular look great as reversible quilts with reversible bindings. Any quilt with a top and underside in completely different fabrics benefits from a reversible binding. This is one of those techniques where I have had many 'experienced' quilters ask 'how did you do that? ' The sunflower quilt has a reversible binding.

Cutting instructions

Choose two fabrics, one for the top binding and the other for the underside binding. These can be completely contrasting to one another. Measure the length of your quilt on both sides and in the centre. If these measurements are not the same, then use a common measurement as the binding

1 Fold the 1¼″ strip lengthways with right side out and press.

2 Lay the folded strip to the right side of the 1″ strip, raw edges matching. Stitch with a ¼″ seam.

3 Gently press the seam open.

4 Pin the binding to the sides of the quilt. Place the 1″ piece right side down to the top of the quilt. Pin from both ends easing the quilt top to fit the binding. Stitch with a ¼″ seam.

5 Fold the binding over the edge, making sure the seam is along the edge so that neither fabric shows opposite sides. Blind stitch the folded edge to the underside of the quilt.

6 Measure the top and bottom width of your quilt, adding an extra 1″ for turning in raw edge of fabric either end. Check that you have a common measurement. Cut binding strips and sew together as before. Turn under the raw edges at either end before stitching the binding to the quilt.

strips need to be pre-cut the same length for both sides.

For the top side cut two 1″ wide strips the length of your quilt.

For the underside cut two 1¼″ wide strips the length of your quilt.

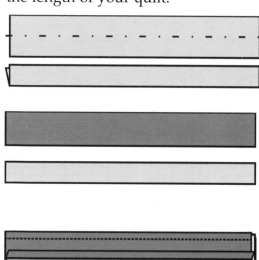

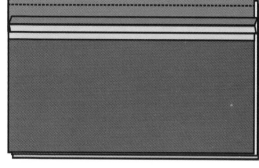

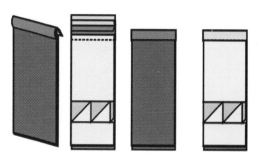

Prairie Points

I have always liked prairie points on the edge of a quilt. They are also fun as a three dimensional extra along a seam inside a quilt.

I have found the traditional method of cutting out squares of fabric, folding and spacing each one precisely a little tedious. Not long after I first started teaching I discovered a continuous band technique which produces prairie points that are evenly spaced and always the same size. The only drawback with this method is that it is unsuitable for a multi-fabric prairie point band.

Prairie points do not need to go all around the quilt. I like to see them on either side of the corners. This avoids any complicated maths in trying to work out the measurements needed to achieve the correct lengths of band for the quilt sides.

If you are adding prairie points all round a quilt then oversize your final border. Once you have made four lengths of prairie points, pin them into position and reduce the border to fit! (I'm avoiding maths again.) The measurements I have given produce a band with finished triangles 1¾" high and 3½" wide along the base.

1 Cut an 8" wide strip of fabric the length you need plus 8" extra. This strip can be pieced. Wrong sides together, fold the strip in half lengthways, press well.

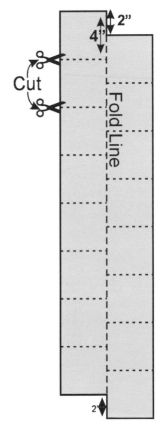

2 Open up the strip. On the wrong side, beginning at the bottom edge, mark off 4"sections. At the top edge, starting 2" in again mark off 4" sections. The 2" x 4" initial section is cut away.

3 Cut on the marked lines from the outer edges to the centre fold line. Do not cut past the centre line.

4 Work on the ironing board, placing the fabric right side down.

5 Start with the nearest square to you, fold as in the diagrams. Continue folding alternating from side to side until all squares are folded and pinned. Pin each point into position after pressing. The finished points should enclose half of the base of the previous point.

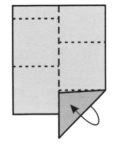
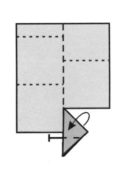
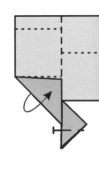

96

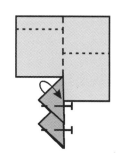
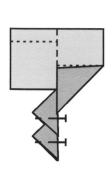
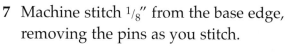
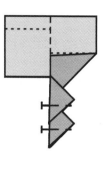

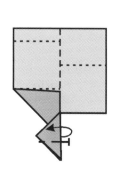

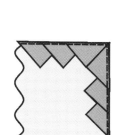

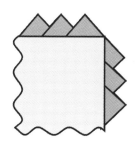

7 Machine stitch ⅛″ from the base edge, removing the pins as you stitch.

8 Pin the prairie point band in place on the right side of the quilt, matching raw edges and with the backing folded away. At the corners the points must lie exactly alongside one another, fitting together.

9 Sew through the prairie points, quilt top and wadding with a ¼″ seam. Trim wadding close to stitching. Fold over the raw edge of the quilt backing and slip stitch into place. If you have used the sew and flip method of assembling the quilt seams that come right to the edge will have to finish ¼″ from the edge to allow the quilt edges to be folded under.

10 Fold the points away from the quilt and hand stitch the backing in place along the seam line on the back.

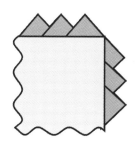

If the triangle bases are not enclosed each time you will have one side that looks like prairie points and the other side will look like 'tulips' – I find this variation attractive.

What if...

You wanted to alternate the points using two different fabrics? Cut a 4¼″ strip from each of the two fabrics. Pin right sides together along the length and stitch with a ¼″ seam. Press the seam open. Then continue cutting and folding from instruction 2.

Double Fold Binding

This is now probably the most common binding used for quilts.

1 Tack through all the layers $1/8''$ from the edge to keep all the layers together.

2 Cut $2\frac{1}{4}''$ strips from your chosen binding fabric on lengthways or crosswise grain of fabric. I prefer to use the lengthways grain as it does not stretch. Occasionally, I find the binding looks better if it is cut from the crosswise grain of a striped or plaid fabric.

3 Join the binding strips together by placing them perpendicular end to end, right sides together. Stitch diagonally with a $\frac{1}{4}''$ seam and press seams open. Join the strips until you have a length equal to the quilt circumference plus $18''$.

4 Cut the beginning of the binding at a 45° angle. Turn in the edge $\frac{1}{4}''$ and press.

5 Fold the binding strip in half lengthwise, wrong sides together and press.

6 Place the binding on the right side of the quilt, aligning raw edges of the binding and the quilt. My starting point is on the bottom quilt edge approximately 6" away from a corner.

7 Using a walking foot begin sewing 2" from the strip end and stopping $\frac{1}{4}''$ from the first quilt corner, back stitch.

8 Remove the quilt from the machine and cut the threads.

9 Fold the binding up, then back down so that the fold is even with the quilt edge. Pin.

10 Begin stitching at the edge of the next side, back stitching to secure the threads. Continue sewing to the next corner. Repeat at all four corners.

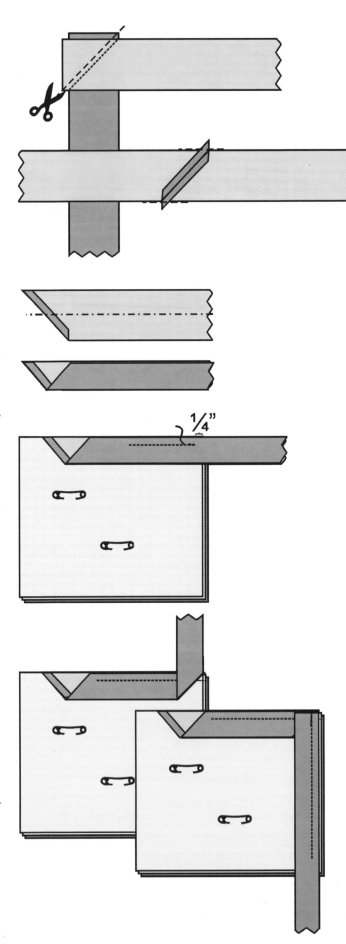

11 As you near the start point, cut the binding strip and tuck the end into the folded strip. Finish the sewing and back stitch.

12 Blind stitch the folded edge to the tucked strip.

13 Turn the binding to the back of the quilt and blind stitch to the backing, covering the previous stitching. Fold the corners as shown.

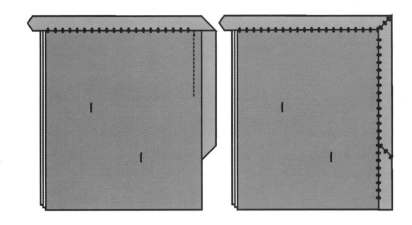

The Sleeve

A sleeve is sewn to the back of the quilt so that it can be easily hung. You may think that this only applies to wall hangings but I recommend that it is done for all quilts as they can then be exhibited without any stress to the quilt. I have known a quilt to be nailed to a piece of wood at a local church display!

1 For bed size quilts, cut a strip of fabric 9" wide and long enough to fit the width of the quilt. A 7" width is suitable for a smaller quilt. Choose fabric that is the same as the backing, or blends well.

2 Turn under ends ¼", press and then turn ½", press, and stitch the turning down.

3 Right sides together, sew into a tube along the length.

4 Iron the seam open. Turn the sleeve through to the right side.

6 Press the sleeve, with good crease lines at the top and bottom and the seam in the centre.

7 Slip stitch the top of the sleeve just under the final binding.

8 Before stitching the bottom of the sleeve, move this edge up ¼" so the sleeve billows slightly. The excess helps the quilt hang better when a wooden pole is inserted into the sleeve.

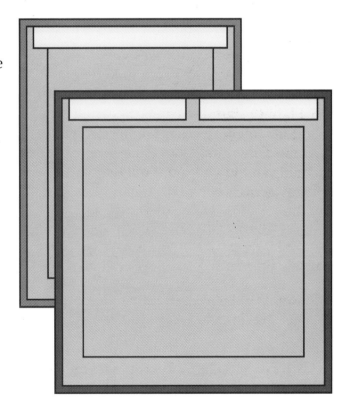

Quilt sleeves help to ensure that a quilt is hung properly, with as little stress as possible. For larger quilts a sleeve that is split in the middle is often an advantage.

Signing your work

As all artists have done over the ages, sign your work! You may not think your quilt is worthy of a label but others will, and it could survive for future social historians to discover and ponder over. The very least you should 'write' on your label is your name, the date the quilt was completed (the year will do) and where the quilt was made (county / state / country will do).

Choose how you are going to 'write' the label. The simplest method is to stabilise a piece of fabric with freezer paper and use a pigma pen to write the details.

If you enjoy embroidery, consider using a back stitch or daisy stitch to outline the writing. A sophisticated sewing machine can be programmed to write and embellish the label.

Labels can also written on the computer and then printed onto computer fabric – why not include a photograph of yourself?

Quilt Care

I use my quilts on beds, walls, wrapped around kids, as teaching aids and displayed in shows. My quilts are well used but I don't find they need frequent cleaning.

If they get dusty, give them a shake outdoors. If the quilt fits comfortably in the washing machine then wash on the gentlest wash cycle with a mild detergent. The larger quilts can be washed by hand in the bath. Lay a sheet under the quilt in the bath as it helps to support the wet quilt when lifting it out. Lay it out flat to dry. If you're drying your quilt outside, choose a shady area; if you're drying indoors, put some towels underneath it.

Keep the quilt out of direct sunlight as this can fade the colours. Fabrics from different sources fade at different rates; some will look like new, but others may lose much of their colour. One quilt hung in the front, south-facing window at Quilters Haven throughout a sunny August (yes, we do get them in Suffolk!) faded beautifully all over giving it an antique look. The fabrics in this quilt were all from the same range and faded at the same rate, a happy accident.

Quilts are best stored laid on a bed or rolled around a tube, right side out. If you have to store them folded, vary the folds after each use. Try layering acid-free tissue paper between folds to protect the quilt.

Projects

His – a beginner's sampler

Design by John Hazon

4" Greek Key (p.28)

4" Courthouse Steps (p.26)

4" Flying Geese (p.40)

4" Patchwork Path (p.46)

4" Chequer board (p.20) and Quarter Square Triangles (p.34)

4" Roman Stripes (p.24)

This is a very straightforward project made up entirely of 4" blocks. The original (see p.112) was a first-time quilt by John Hazon, who was fascinated by the Sew a Row concept and just had to have a go!

Each of the 4" rows consists of 6 blocks, usually all the same; however, row 3 has a continuous skein of geese, and row 5 alternates chequer board and quarter square triangles. 1" strips separate the rows (cut strips 1½" wide). Use your favourite blocks. Select colours you like, and play!

QH Tip

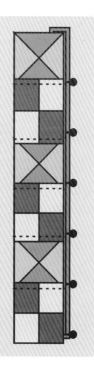

Measure the length of those sashing strips and mark 4" intervals with pins. As you sew on the blocks you can ease minor discrepancies in the piecing (as shown here) clean out of the way!

Olde Worlde

Design by Karin Hellaby

C'house steps	Dresden Daisy	C'house steps
C'house steps	Dresden Diamond	C'house steps
C'house steps	Dresden Daisy	C'house steps
C'house steps	Dresden Diamond	C'house steps

This quilt was designed to hang over the back of a rocking chair. The original (see p. 109) is made completely of 8″ blocks. The central row uses alternating Dresden Daisies (see p. 70) and Dresden Diamonds (p. 72) that have been appliquéd onto pieced 8½″ squares. It is flanked on either side by an 8″ row of Courthouse Steps.

Use these blocks (or others that appeal to you) in colours that suit your decor! The prairie points make a stunning edging but you could use simple binding, especially if you planned to use it as a baby mat rather than a rocking chair throw.

Sunflowers – a reversible quilt

Designed by Pam Bailey

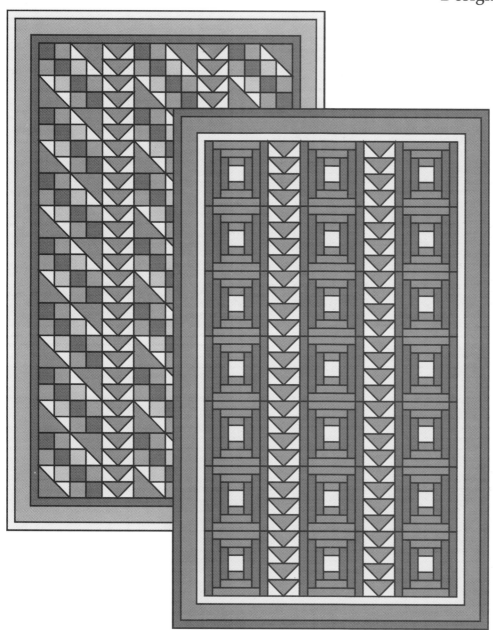

Pam Bailey named her quilt from the fabric she used in nearly all the blocks on both sides of her reversible quilt. This pretty sunflower print helped her choose the other colours she used (see p.16) and the two sides of the quilt are carefully coordinated.

You could, however, use completely different colour schemes for either side of your quilt: the reversible binding (see p.95) could complete, for example, a range of spring and contrasting autumn (fall) colours. You could use ice cream colours on one side and disco colours on the other – the important thing is to choose rows that add up! Eight 4" rows on one side exactly match the three 8" plus two 4" rows on the other.

As for the blocks, the first side (in the background here) uses Squared-up Triangles (p.36) alternating with Chequer Boards (p.20), and separated by two rows of Flying Geese (p.40), while the other side uses the same Flying Geese rows to separate three 8" strips of Courthouse Steps (p.26).

Harvest Home – a simple throw

Designed by Karin Hellaby

The perfect picnic quilt...
Made in homespun
flannels, using Quarter
Square Triangles (p.34)
and plain squares in 4"
blocks, and bordered
using a quick strip pieced
border (p.85). Karin's
original quilt (see p.109) is
backed with fleece and
tied with cross-stitch.

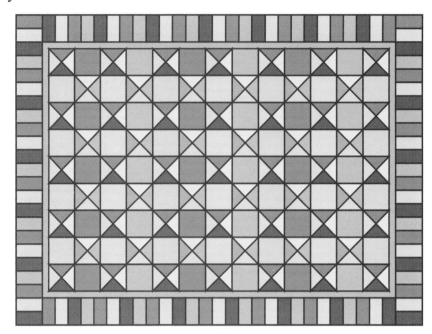

Autumn Splendour – a full-sized quilt

Designed by Clare Dunderdale

Autumn Splendour , like
other quilts in this book,
takes its name from the
colours and fabrics Clare
has chosen to make it. It
shows off the Sew a Row
idea to perfection, in a
nicely symmetrical, full-
sized quilt.

The central 8" row of Greek
Keys (p.28) is flanked on
either side by an 8" row of
Squared-up Triangles (p.36),
Tulips (pp.49-51) and
Courthouse Steps (p.26),
with an outer 4" row of
Flying Geese (p.40).

Designed by Pat Boyes

A more advanced quilt, but one that uses the Sew a Row Magic Formula to real advantage. You can see Pat's finished quilt on p.110.

The central 8″ row is dominated by Chop Suey blocks (see p.22); interesting variations give a very arresting focus to the quilt. On either side are 2″ plain strips of fabric, separating it from three 4″ rows that make inventive use of Courthouse Steps (p.26) and 3D Geese (p.39).

Pat has varied the number of Courthouse Step blocks in each row, and used one fabric to make up the length. By swinging round the orientation of the blocks, she creates a fascinating diagonal drift that combines oriental magic with a sense of deep tranquillity.

Flight of Fancy

Design by Pat Boyes

This one is definitely an advanced project! You can see Pat's finished quilt on p.90, but this diagram shows the structure. The centre 4″ row consists of Dancing Squares (see p.52), bordered on either side with a 2″ strip decorated with bias tape appliqué (see p.82), a 4″ row featuring skinny triangles (see p.35), and a final 4″ row featuring 'half' Dresden Daisies (see p.70).

The simple tonal range of this diagram does not do justice to the subtlety of the colours in Pat's hanging. You can use a colour wash effect similar to hers, or you can do your own thing! Pat has mixed cotton with silk to superb effect.

This could make a spectacular Christmas hanging, or even a table runner.

Further reading

Fabric Shopping by Alex Anderson, C & T, ISBN 1-57120089-4

Quilters' Ultimate Visual Guide by Ellen Pahl, Rodale Press, ISBN 0-87596710-8

Measure the Possibilities with Omnigrid by Nancy Johnson-Srebro, Silver Star Inc., ISBN 0-96387640-6

Make any Block any Size by Joen Wolfron, C & T, ISBN 1-57120068-1

Easy Machine Paper Piecing by Carol Doak, That Patchwork Place, ISBN 1-56477038-9

The Appliqué Handbook by Goldsmith & Jenkins, Piece O'Cake Designs

Artful Appliqué by Jane Townswick, That Patchwork Place, ISBN 1-56477038-9

Mastering Machine Appliqué by Harriet Hargrave, C & T, ISBN 0-91488145-0

Invisible Machine Appliqué by Dawn Cameron-Dick, Teamwork Craftbooks, ISBN 0-95325902-1

Quilt It by Barbara Chainey, That Patchwork Place, ISBN 1-56477075-3

Learn to do Hand Quilting in just one Day by Nancy Brennan Daniel, American School of Needlework, ISBN 0-88195783-6

Heirloom Machine Quilting by Harriet Hargrave, C & T, ISBN 0-91488192-2

Acknowledgements

Distribution outside the UK

Quilters' Resource Inc
PO Box 148850
Chicago
Illinois 60614
USA

Tel: 312-278-5795

Custom machine quilting

Quilting Solutions
Firethorn, Rattlesden Road
Drinkstone
Bury St Edmunds
Suffolk IP30 9TL
UK

Tel: 01449 736280

www.quiltingsolutions.co.uk

Designs from *Electric Quilt 4*

Electric Quilt Company
419 Gould Street, Suite 2
Bowling Green
OH 43402
USA

Tel: 419-352-1134

www.wcnet.org/ElectricQuiltCo/

Layout and Design
Allen Scott and Rosemary Muntus
Old Mill House
The Causeway
Hitcham
Suffolk IP7 7NF UK

Tel: 01449 741747

www.muntus.co.uk

Index

Sew a Row Quilts

Sew a Row Funtime *by Anne Smith (64" x 80")
is just that – no borders needed for* this *quilt!*

Autumn Splendour *by Clare Dunderdale (66"x 72") was the first quilt to be layered using 'sew and flip (see p.88). Clare loved the technique and was surprised how easy it was to do.*

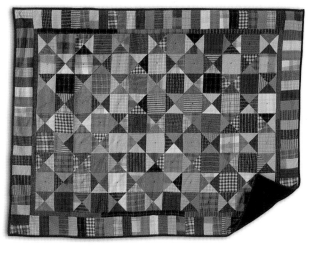

Olde Worlde *by Karin Hellaby (27"x 34") has a multi-fabric background. As Karin says, 'why use one cream when several will do?'*

Harvest Home, *a rug by Karin Hellaby (55" x 66"), is backed with fleece and tied with cross stitch.*

Incomplete rows give an eastern look to Shades of the Orient, *a wall hanging by Pat Boyes (32"x 55"). Pat hand quilted her work with big stitches to create a sashiko effect.*

Silken Climbers *by Anne Smith (29"x 42") makes clever use of hearts to give the effect of butterfly wings.*

Rows by any other name *(63"x 79") was pieced and quilted by Jan Chandler of Quilting Solutions.*

Confetti Hearts *(27"x 29") by Lin Patterson.*
Hand-dyed fabrics help the colours break away from
the simple row formula.

Cover quilt What If? *by Claire Frew (49"x 68") – a*
vibrant and imaginative use of colour, and of the
Sew a Row technique.

Sunflowers *by Pam Bailey (39" x 63") is a reversible lap quilt*
finished with reversible binding (see p.95), pieced by Pam and machine
quilted by Quilting Solutions.

His (left, 30"x 36") 'n Hers (86"x 100"), by John and Helen Hazon, are living examples of a rare form of togetherness. John had never tried quiltmaking until he read the notes Helen was following. Now he is making his second quilt. Helen's large quilt was easily put together using the sew and flip technique. It needs no further quilting, but Helen says she may go back to hand quilt it.

About the author

Karin Hellaby was born in the north-east of England of Norwegian parents: her first language was Norwegian. She studied for a Home Economics teaching degree from the University of Wales. Now she lives in Suffolk, and is the single parent of three wonderful boys.

Karin started teaching quiltmaking around her kitchen table when pregnant with her third son, Alexander, who is now 11 years old. Quilters Haven opened in 1993 as a teaching centre, with a shop alongside to supply the students, a unique concept in England at that time. It moved to its 17th-century timber-framed building in 1996. The attractive shop, with gallery room and teaching area, attracts quiltmakers and teachers from all over the world. In 1998 Karin, with the help of her son Ross (then aged 15), won the Kile Scholarship – International Retailer of the Year. The next step was to write a book... and here it is!